RUFUS WAINWRIGHT

Popular Music History

Series Editor: Alyn Shipton, Royal Academy of Music, London, and City University, London

This series publishes books that challenge established orthodoxies in popular music studies, examine the formation and dissolution of canons, interrogate histories of genres, focus on previously neglected forms, or engage in archaeologies of popular music.

Published

RUFUS WAINWRIGHT

KATHERINE WILLIAMS

SHEFFIELD UK   BRISTOL CT

Published by Equinox Publishing Ltd.

UK: Office 415, The Workstation, 15 Paternoster Row, Sheffield, South Yorkshire S1 2BX
USA: ISD, 70 Enterprise Drive, Bristol, CT 06010

www.equinoxpub.com

First published 2016

© Katherine Williams 2016

All rights reserved. No part of this publication may be reproduced or transmitted in
any form or by any means, electronic or mechanical, including photocopying, recording or any information storage or retrieval system, without prior permission in writing from the publishers.

British Library Cataloguing-in-Publication Data
A catalogue record for this book is available from the British Library.

Library of Congress Cataloging-in-Publication Data
Williams, Katherine (Katherine Ann)
 Rufus Wainwright / Katherine Williams.
    pages cm. -- (Popular music history)
 Includes bibliographical references and index.
 ISBN 978-1-84553-293-2 (hb)
 1. Wainwright, Rufus, 1973- 2. Singers--United States--Biography. 3.
Composers--United States--Biography. 4. Lyricists--United
States--Biography. I. Title.
 ML420.W126W55 2016
 782.42164092--dc23
 [B]
                                    2015030878

ISBN: 978 1 84553 293 2 (hardback)

Typeset by CA Typesetting Ltd, www.publisherservices.co.uk
Printed and bound in the UK by Lightning Source UK Ltd., Milton Keynes and
Lightning Source Inc., La Vergne, TN

Contents

List of Figures and Tables

Acknowledgements

The author is grateful to the following publishers for permission to quote extracts from the following songs:

Kobalt Songs Music Publishing, 'Beauty Mark', 'Imaginary Love', 'Greek Song'.
Warner Chappell Music, 'Dinner at Eight', 'Pretty Things', 'Vibrate', 'Candles', 'Want'.
Bärenreiter-Verlag Karl Vötterle GmbH & Co. KG, 'Ave Maria'.

I researched and wrote this book with support from my fellow scholars, friends and family. My husband Justin (aka Dr Hip-Hop) has been a powerhouse of strength and support, and has always, ALWAYS, believed in my ability to write this and produce something of interest and value. He has listened to my ideas throughout, and proofread the entire manuscript at a late stage. The first and biggest thank you goes to Justin, to whom this book is dedicated with love and respect.

I first heard Rufus Wainwright's music during my MA in Musicology at the University of Nottingham. The film *Brokeback Mountain* had been released a few years earlier, and Professor Paula Higgins was in the process of preparing her paper for the 2008 meeting of the American Musicological Society. "Stemming the Rose, Queering the Pitch: The Cultural Politics of Rufus Wainwright's 'The Maker Makes'" introduced me to a new voice, and opened my eyes and ears to the possibility of in-depth scholarship on aspects of popular culture.

I continually reflect thankfully on my experiences as a PhD student at Nottingham with Professor Mervyn Cooke. His wisdom and good nature have set a precedent for the way I handle my work and my own students, and he continues his role as mentor – albeit informally and remotely these days! I am grateful to my external examiner Professor Tony Whyton. After interrogating me on my PhD, which examined the fruitful use of classical music in jazz in the Anglophone world, he asked whether I had considered applying a similar framework to popular music. This book is one of the results.

During the research period for this book, I was fortunate to present my findings at several conferences. My thanks go to the delegates, panel members and chair people of the OBERTO "Operatic Masculinities" Study Day (Oxford Brookes, September 2012); "The Singer-Songwriter in Europe" (University of

Leeds, September 2012); popMAC (University of Liverpool, July 2013); "Music Since 1900" (Liverpool Hope University, September 2013); Royal Musical Association annual conference (Institute of Musical Research, London, September 2013); "Verdi's Third Century" (New York University, October 2013); International Association for the Study of Popular Music (University College Cork, Ireland, September 2014); and EuroMAC (Leuven University, Belgium, September 2014). Each of these conferences was a fruitful and intellectually stimulating experience, and I am grateful for the formal questions and informal interest that scholars took in my work. I have acknowledged particularly pertinent individual contributions as they arise in my text.

My thanks to superb readers of draft material: Dr Alex Wilson showed patience and expertise by reading very early drafts of Chapters 2 and 3. Dr Joe Bennett provided useful feedback on Chapter 2 from a popular music and songwriting perspective. Dr Carlo Cenciarelli offered his insights into Chapter 4, and I am grateful also to Carlo for the many minimalist operas we attended together, for the lengthy debates about musicology and life, and for the friendship. Dr Ruth Dockwray applied her expertise to my readings of the tracks analysed in Chapter 5, and created the sound-box diagrams. Ruth gave her time and advice freely, and I am particularly grateful for this generous application of a methodology that she initially helped develop for a different repertoire. I am grateful also to Dr Michael Ellison, Jonathan Scott, Rob Northcott and Arthur Keegan-Bole at the University of Bristol, who offered alternative opinions on troubling song analyses in Chapter 5. Jonathan Scott also showed extraordinary patience with my endless questions about recording equipment and studio techniques.

Several friends that I made along the pathway to fully-fledged academic have developed their own careers as professional musicians. I sought professional advice on operatic ranges from freelance opera singer Lorna James (who has enjoyed lengthy stints with prestigious companies, and recently returned from playing Musetta in Opera North's *La Bohème*). Freelance accompanist and vocal coach Sonum Batra applied her knowledge of vocal techniques in musical theatre to help me with the proxemic analyses I carry out in Chapter 4.

I am grateful to my students at Leeds College of Music for indulging my initial ideas about this topic. This book started life as a series of case studies used to explain classical and popular music theories and methodologies to students from both disciplines, and students at LCoM (Years 1 and 2, 2011–2013) bore with me while I developed theories. Their patience with my repeated questioning ("what do you hear?", "what do you *really* hear?", "what do you think that means?") deserves recognition.

Thanks to Clifford Allen, of the Watermill Center in New York, for helping me obtain access to films of the *Sonnette* performances. Thanks to members of the IASPM listserv for suggesting ways of obtaining the BBC documentary discussed in Chapter 2. The editorial and production team at Equinox have been supportive and patient throughout. My thanks in particular to David Laing, Janet Joyce, Val Hall and Alyn Shipton.

But of course, my greatest thanks and respect go to Rufus Wainwright. I was fortunate enough to meet him in July 2013 when I was attending the popMAC conference in Liverpool. Many delegates (including myself) attended a party to celebrate twenty-five years of the Institute of Popular Music, held at the Leaf Bar in Liverpool. The IPM had hired out the upper floor of the venue for the party, and the lower floor was dedicated to an amateur singer-songwriter open mic. Rumours started circulating that Rufus Wainwright was downstairs, and I was encouraged by several colleagues to go and investigate. I did so – Rufus was standing at the bar with songwriter Guy Chambers. I have never seen a person exude so much stardom before: he had a loud speaking voice, and a dynamic and charismatic personality that was evident even from across the room. I introduced myself, explained that I am a fan of his work, and explained the current project. Rufus Wainwright endorsed the book wholeheartedly – I count myself lucky to have encountered him by chance, and to have had such a positive outcome.

This book is inspired by Rufus Wainwright's music, and by his colourful life story. A project such as this must be contained in some way, so I have chosen to end my period of focus after his seventh studio album, *Out of the Game*. Nonetheless, I have watched his developments since with interest, and I wish him the greatest of success in his future endeavours.

Katherine Williams
Bristol, October 2015

Introduction

"Oh What a World"

Rufus Wainwright and his backing singers file on to the stage, helped by anonymous stagehands. The backing singers begin humming a wordless melody. This tranquility is short-lived, with the addition of a tuba bassline marking out both the duple pulse and the tonality, alternating between the tonic and the dominant below. "Showbiz", Wainwright announces, over the hummed melody. The Canadian-American singer-songwriter stands at the front of the stage, half-conducting, half-swaying to the music ("I'm a *fabulous* dancer", he observes). "Men reading fashion magazines", he sings, dressed in a t-shirt and a pale linen suit. The outfit is finished with a floor-length black witch's cape and a witch's hat – adornments shared by the on-stage backing singers and band. "Oh what a world it seems we live in", he observes, indirectly explaining his costume, and his position in society.[1]

"Oh what a world" is the Wicked Witch of the West's cry, as Dorothy douses her in water, causing her to melt at the end of L. Frank Baum's classic novel from 1900, *The Wonderful Wizard of Oz*. The book, and more accurately, Judy Garland, star of the 1939 Metro-Goldwyn-Mayer film adaptation, have long been considered gay classics, and symbolic icons of gay culture.[2] By choosing this as his refrain, Wainwright acknowledges both his longstanding obsession with musical theatre and his own involvement in a gay lifestyle, as well as commenting upon contemporary society (and implicitly, his perception and rejection of stereotypical American attitudes towards homosexuality). He continues: "Straight men [often interjecting a sardonic 'right' in performance], oh what a world we live in".

The second verse of 'Oh What a World' is marked musically by the addition of a deadened tom-tom hit on the first beat of each bar. Wainwright segues forward, querying the effort and commitment necessitated by the quest for fame and celebrity. "Oh what a world my parents gave me", he continues—Loudon Wainwright III and Kate McGarrigle were both folk stars in their own right before meeting on the New York coffeehouse circuit in the late 1960s, and marrying in 1971.

Wainwright's performance of 'Oh What a World' continues into the third verse. The humming chorus returns, now supported by the tuba and percussion backdrop. Wainwright reiterates the three verses, now announced by a cymbal crash, echoed by backing singers, and accompanied by ascending and descending pizzicato string figures. The second iteration of the final verse features an orchestral statement of the famous theme from Maurice Ravel's 'Bolero'. The combination of Wainwright's indie-pop influenced lead vocal, the musical theatre-influenced backdrop, and the loud, brassy orchestral melody emphasize Wainwright's varied musical origins. He flings his arms out, conducting, dancing, and rejoicing in the music he knows and that he has created. The textures grow with the additions of swelling strings and repeats of the 'Bolero' theme. Ravel's solo woodwind statements are accompanied by descending string figures. Wainwright acts out the fall of the Wicked Witch, swaying and circling to the ground as the music fades.

Wainwright's use of Ravel's music, and the formal suit that he wears underneath his flamboyant cape, betray a concern with traditions from western art music. The juxtaposition of these two art worlds is a central feature of this book. The journalist and music critic Simon Hattenstone described Wainwright as "one of the world's most acclaimed singer-songwriters ... [who] ultimately [would] like to be judged against Wagner and Verdi and Mozart" (Hattenstone, 2007).

Is it possible for the same person to be an esteemed popular music singer-songwriter and an adherent of the western art music tradition? Rufus Wainwright's music and persona prompts extreme responses: whether positive or negative, reactions are always strong. Wainwright's work lends itself to critical methods drawn from both the classical and popular music fields. He is a colourful and enigmatic performing figure, whose frequent media interviews and autobiographical songs allow insight into his personality and personal history. In addition, his music, performances and stage persona can be deconstructed to lend a prism through which to view several disciplinary frameworks.

Indeed, the "other side" of Wainwright's artistic personality is clearly demonstrated by another performance of 'Oh What a World'. On the final night of a week-long residency at the Royal Opera House in London in July 2011, he presented an alternative version of himself in character as an art-music composer. The first half of the concert had consisted of a stage version of extracts from his first opera *Prima Donna*, accompanied by the Britten Sinfonia. Wainwright was clearly visible throughout the first half, watching the performance carefully from a box. The second half of the performance consisted of Wainwright performing his original popular songs. The orchestra remained on stage, as Wainwright joined them, dressed in a stylish dark suit, his exuberance marked only by an oversized white scarf. The setting, live orchestral accompaniment, and Wainwright's sartorial decisions and earnest attitude, all combined to imply an art-music performance. Yet the musical and verbal content remained that of popular music, providing an example of varied perspectives on the same material allowing different interpretations. "Oh What a World", he sings.

Despite Wainwright's fame and artistry, little published material focuses on his life and music. Journalistic interviews tend to deal with his openness about his lifestyle and family. *There Will Be Rainbows: A Biography of Rufus Wainwright* (an unofficial life story by UK-based journalist Kirk Lake) spends a considerable amount of time on the story of Loudon and Kate's relationship, and explores the careers of the entire family and the family dynamic. Lake briefly describes Wainwright's songs in the order in which they appear on the albums, but being primarily a celebrity biography it is frugal in musical detail. Oliver C. E. Smith's "'The Cult of the Diva': Rufus Wainwright as Opera Queen" appeared in the French-language journal *Transpositions: musiques et science sociales* in March 2013.

There are two postgraduate dissertations on Rufus Wainwright's music but neither has been published in any form (Jones, 2002; Schwandt, 2010). Some scholarly output comes from a lesbian, gay, bisexual, transsexual and queer (LGBTQ) standpoint. However, I write as a heterosexual female, and intend to consider his career and output as examples to illustrate wider issues in musicology and critical theory. Consideration of queer theory and gendered perspectives is but one of several approaches used here. My focus is art music and popular music existing together, and song analysis from a variety of standpoints.

Biographical Overview

Wainwright claims always to have known that he was homosexual, and two important events occurred in his fourteenth year: he came out as gay to his parents, and he discovered the life and music of Giuseppe Verdi (1813– 1903). From that point the nineteenth-century Italian opera composer featured heavily in Wainwright's life, both as a figurehead and as a musical inspiration. Thus began the two musical worlds of Wainwright's career: he made his name as an indie pop singer-songwriter, but western art music has always featured heavily in his output. He accompanies himself on the piano, with background parts that are often virtuosic (only infrequently choosing to accompany himself on the more stereotypical pop instrument, the guitar), and he has always chosen producers who will indulge his penchant for multiple layers of orchestral sound, even on studio albums that are ostensibly pop. Lyrical references to western art music figures are frequent, ranging from the composer Schubert ('Imaginary Love') to operatic heroines ('Damned Ladies').

The trajectory of Wainwright's studio output shows an oscillation between attempts at crowd-pleasing commercial pop and the "elaborate, baroque stylings of his debut album" (Lake, 2009: 175), which catered more to his art music sensibility. In 1995, after several years of paying his dues on the cabaret circuits in New York and Montreal, Rufus Wainwright recorded a demo with acclaimed Canadian producer Pierre Marchand, who had previously produced albums for Kate and Anna McGarrigle.

Through family contacts, Wainwright sent his demo to producers Van Dyke Parks and Lenny Waronker. A contract with the newly founded Dream-Works Records followed in January 1996. Executives at the company had been so impressed with his live performances that his then-manager Nick Terzo explains that they granted him a budget of $1 million to cover all expenditure on his first two albums (Lake, 2009: 124). For his debut album *Rufus Wainwright* (1998), he recorded 62 reels of tape with producer Jon Brion. The album featured multiple layers of orchestral sound and cost $750,000 to make (Robinson, 2005). The record was unsuccessful in commercial terms, selling only 55,000 copies in the United States, and failing to chart. However, the album gained critical acclaim: Wainwright won "Best New Artist" in *Rolling Stone*, the album made the *Village Voice* top 10 albums of the year, and he got plaudits from critics including the influential Robert Christgau (Christgau 1998). This balance between artistic recognition from the cognoscenti and underwhelming commercial success was to continue throughout Wainwright's studio career. (A fuller version of these events is contained in Chapter 1.)

Despite the minimal popular success he achieved, Wainwright's Dream-Works contract was binding, and he needed to recoup some money for the company. In May 2001, he announced his intention "to scale it down a little, and make it more accessible. I'm going to write a huge pop album that's going to sell millions of copies and going to be all hit songs." He remarked on the commonly understood dichotomy between artistic value and commercial success, remarking in the same interview: "I'm totally selling out" (Wainwright in Graff, 2001). Wainwright recorded his second album in Canada with producer Pierre Marchand, and *Poses* was released in June 2001. Wainwright's use of devices from the popular music world is overt, with conventional pop song forms, beats, loops, synthesized sounds and catchy hooks. This approach achieved the desired commercial effect, and *Poses* debuted at number 117 on the Billboard 200. Again, contemporary reviewers commented favourably on Wainwright's artistry and musicianship: for example, the *New Music Express*'s John Robinson praised the "maniacal attention to detail and conceptual strength" (2005). *Poses* is bookended by two versions of Wainwright's song 'Cigarettes and Chocolate Milk', which not only provides an example of his popular songwriting style and vocal range (for example, the opening line spans a major ninth), but offers an insight into his biography. Almost all his songs are written with the first person pronoun, and refer to incidents in his life, many of which he discusses in media interviews. 'Cigarettes and Chocolate Milk' is no different, referring to "just a few of [his] cravings" when embracing the pop-star lifestyle in New York's Chelsea Hotel. (During the writing and production of *Poses*, Wainwright lived variously at the Chelsea Hotel in Manhattan, and in Los Angeles. He stayed at the Gramercy Park Hotel in Manhattan while promoting the album.)

During this period (2001–2002), Wainwright became dependent on alcohol and drugs. After a series of chaotic health scares and manic behaviour (including temporarily going blind from crystal meth use at one point, and demanding a tour of Yoko Ono's house at an antisocial hour at another), on the advice of friend and sometime mentor Elton John he checked into rehab in the Hazeldon Clinic in Minneapolis. Wainwright had begun work on a third album with producer Marius de Vries, and he continued writing material throughout his rehabilitation and recovery. During an intense burst of creativity in January 2003, Wainwright recorded thirty tracks. He titled the sessions *Want*, and they marked a return to the elaborate and opulent style of his first album. At this point, DreamWorks was undergoing financial problems, and although Wainwright had conceived and recorded *Want* as a large-scale double album, he eventually agreed to release the material in two stages. (DreamWorks was incorporated into Geffen Records in 2004.) Wainwright divided the material thematically into autobiographical songs with straightforward narratives on *Want One* (released 2003), and darker, more psychologically complex material on *Want Two* (2004). *Want One* reached number 60 on the US Billboard 200, exceeding *Poses*' 117. *Want Two* showed a decline in commercial popularity in America, reaching number 103 on the Billboard 200. However, *Want Two* entered the British charts at number 21, marking Wainwright's first major success in the European market.

Wainwright's breakout success (relative to his previous records) was 2007's *Release the Stars*, which peaked at number 2 in the British charts, and number 23 in the US Billboard 200. After the extravagance of the *Want* albums, Wainwright intended *Release the Stars* to be a more streamlined pop venture, an idea reinforced by enlisting the help of Pet Shop Boy Neil Tennant as executive producer. He also undertook some of the production work himself, with the help of engineer Tom Schick. Working in Berlin, he initially planned a solo piano and voice album in the style of art song. His 2001 interview with Michael Giltz in *The Advocate* suggests that he had been stockpiling "American Lieder, totally Straussian, Schubertian, very Germanic" for some time, but had previous felt that "America wasn't ready for them yet" (Wainwright in

Giltz, 2001: 39). The operatic and European leanings evidenced in *Rufus Wain-wright* and the *Want* albums again resurfaced in the Germanic environment, where he had access to some of the top freelance classical musicians in the world. Although the songs on the album primarily use standard pop forms, by using classical session musicians, and through musical and extra-musical references, *Release the Stars* brought together the two aspects of his life. The album was Wainwright's most commercially successful album to date, selling over 100,000 copies in the UK.

At this time, Wainwright also expanded his ambitions and activities on the western art music platform. Another reason for Wainwright's diversion from the planned pop-centric album in 2007 was the fact that Peter Gelb, the new head of the Metropolitan Opera in New York, had recently commissioned him to write an opera. This project, which marked the culmination of several of Wainwright's musical and lifestyle hopes and ambitions, took up a good deal of his time and naturally affected the musical direction of his existing projects. Wainwright followed in the Wagnerian tradition by writing the libretto, as well as the music, himself. His decision to write in French made it ultimately unsuitable for the Metropolitan Opera, who were hoping for a contemporary English language opera, and *Prima Donna* was eventually premiered in Britain as part of the Manchester International Festival in 2009.

Wainwright continued the alternation of art-music inflected albums with commercially oriented records with the spartan, lieder-inspired *All Days Are Nights: Songs for Lulu* (2010). The reduction of instrumental forces was partly a financial decision; Wainwright toured alone, as declining ticket prices forced him to perform without a band (Everett-Green, 2010). Wainwright stripped the textures down to solo piano and voice, and produced the album himself with Marchand's help. By promoting the album as a song cycle, albeit within popular music marketing strategies, Wainwright's two musical worlds came together firmly – but the sales statistics show that the commercial audience did not respond well to the artistic blending of two worlds. *All Days Are Nights* charted at number 75 in the US Billboard 200, and number 21 in the UK. This was his first album to reach the Canadian charts, despite both *Poses* and *Release the Stars* gaining a Gold award there. *All Days Are Nights* charted in Canada at number 4.

His seventh studio album, *Out of the Game*, was produced by Mark Ronson and released in April 2012. Ronson is a well-known music producer with a retro style, and the album is the most overtly pop-centric of Wainwright's output. The title track contains the line "I'm out of the game" – a clear lament for his loss of success in the popular music sphere. The commercial market responded yet again to popular music influences: *Out of the Game* reached number 35 in the Billboard 200, number 5 in the UK chart, and number 11 in the Canadian charts. Despite ongoing projects in both the popular and classical music fields, Rufus Wainwright cannot consistently reconcile his musical personae. Throughout this book, I explore the energy and creativity generated by this conflict.

Methodology

All music analysis refers to a "text", which in western art music is usually the notated score. Locating the text in popular song is more problematic, for there is rarely a definitive score. The influential British popular music scholar Allan Moore observes that a popular song simultaneously exists in three ways: the *song* (harmonic and melodic structure, as might be laid out on a jazz lead sheet), the *performance* (the vocal timbre, instrumentation, and melodic decoration of a particular iteration of the song), and the *track* (a performance of the song, fixed in time by being issued as a recording). The track may also be altered by studio techniques before release (Moore 2012: 15). I adopt Moore's terminology throughout, and in my analyses and observations I refer to the track on the official studio albums, unless otherwise clarified.

My musical examples are intended to be accessible to readers from both popular music and western art music backgrounds, including a combination of score-based transcriptions with notation and bar numbers, tabular analysis of song structure, verbal analyses, and references to track times on identified audio recordings. The transcriptions are not musically quantified from the recorded track, but provide a starting point for a performance of the song, much as a jazz or pop lead sheet provides a simplified melody and chords for performers to interpret as they desire. My combination of notated and non-notated systems of analysis is intended to illustrate the value of a variety of analytical tools.

In the song analyses that follow, I provide tabular analyses of song structure, using the formal delineations suggested by John Covach and Andrew Flory in *What's That Sound?* (2012). The song structures consist of a number of building blocks: the *verse* (usually twelve or sixteen bars, made out of four- or eight-bar phrases), which is repeated with changing lyrics; the *chorus* (a section that repeats the same music and lyrics intact in each presentation); the *bridge* (usually heard once in the entire song, with contrasting musical and verbal content to the verse and chorus); the *refrain* (a section that usually appears at the end of the verse, with contrasting melodic, harmonic and rhythmic content); the *pre-chorus* (which serves a similar function to the refrain, but appears as contrasting material between the verse and chorus); and the *reprise* (when some or all of the song structure is repeated). The most common forms using these building blocks are simple verse form (repeated verses), simple verse-chorus (the same musical content for alternating verse and chorus lyrics), and contrasting verse-chorus (different, though repeated, content for the verse and chorus). These forms may be extended in many ways, often with bridges and pre-choruses.

Any book about a contemporary figure runs the risk of quickly becoming out of date. I have chosen the timeframe under consideration carefully: at the time I began writing in 2012, Wainwright had just released his seventh original studio album. Although he has continued his creative activity (releasing *Vibrate: The Best of Rufus Wainwright* in March 2014, and planning a new opera, *Hadrian*, for performance in 2018), this book focuses on the creative period up to and including *Out of the Game* (2012).

1 Family

The songs that we sing are very sad, they're very intense, they're very serious, they're very personal, they're very revealing.
(Martha Wainwright in Scott, 2009: 1:15:42)

Rufus Wainwright's family has impacted upon his life and career in many ways: from the conventional (Loudon and Kate conceived and raised him), to the vocational (the musical household in Montreal was an ideal place in which to begin a career as a singer-songwriter, and throughout his career members of his family have contributed musically to his output, singing backing vocals or adding instrumental tracks), to the musically referential (Rufus continued a Wainwright and McGarrigle family tradition of expressing sibling and filial relationships through song).[1]

The story of Rufus Wainwright must begin with his parents. Loudon Snowden Wainwright III was born on 5 September 1946, in Chapel Hill, South Carolina. His parents Martha, a yoga teacher, and Loudon Jr, a journalist, were not professional musicians, but Loudon Jr played piano and exposed his children to musicians such as Tom Lehrer and Stan Freberg. Loudon III's youth was spent in Westchester County, NY, New York City and Beverley Hills, CA. Loudon Jr was in charge of the Los Angeles office of *Life* magazine for a short period during this time, and young Loudon met several celebrities (including Liza Minnelli) through his father's work. He began playing the guitar in 1960, and declared Bob Dylan his musical idol after seeing him perform live at the Newport Folk Festival in 1962. After graduating from high school in 1965, Loudon attended Carnegie Mellon drama school in Pittsburgh, although he dropped out in 1967. After a brief diversion to San Francisco to experience the beginnings of the hippy movement, Loudon soon moved back to New York to partake fully in the folk revival. He spent many nights socializing and performing at the Village Gaslight and Gerde's Folk City – venues that helped precipitate Bob Dylan's rise to fame and initial record deal with Columbia in October 1962. Loudon began writing his own folk songs – developing his drily autobiographical signature style – while working at a variety of part-time jobs. As he comments in the biographical section of his website (which is written in the first person), "male singer songwriters were a happening commodity back then", and he was signed to Atlantic Records in 1969. An insight into the autobiographical nature of Loudon's songs can be gained from the biography on his website: each incident in his background is listed with a footnote reference to the song in which he sings about it.[2] His first album, *Loudon Wainwright III*, was released in 1970, and *Album II* the following year.

Kate McGarrigle was born on 6 February 1946 in Montreal, to mixed English and French-Canadian parents. Kate was the youngest of three daughters: although the eldest, Jane, went on to write and perform folk songs with her younger sisters, she worked primarily in music management rather than on the stage. The middle sister, Anna, was born on 4 December 1944. The sisters grew up in the mountain village of Saint-Saveur-des-Monts, Québec, in a household where family music-making was a regular occurrence. In the early 1960s, Kate studied engineering at McGill University in Montreal, while Anna studied painting at L'Ecole des Beaux-Arts in the same city. While studying, the sisters began to write and perform songs as part of the burgeoning Montreal folk scene. After university, Anna took a job with social services in Montreal, while Kate formed a folk duo with an established folk singer friend, Roma Baran. Kate and Roma headed to New York, become part of the city's folk revival scene, eventually playing some of the same clubs as Loudon Wainwright III. Back home in Montreal, Anna continued writing her own folk material, some of which – such as 'Heart Like a Wheel' – she sent to Kate, who included the song in her regular set.

To place Kate and Loudon's music-making in context, it is worth looking back at the tradition in which they worked. Folk music was crucial to the development of national identity in the late 1800s, as rural communities in Europe and North America expressed nationhood and local colour through song.[3] The term "folk" derived from the German "Volk", referring to both people and nation. According to Norm Cohen (n.d.), "folk music" refers to music that has was transmitted orally rather than through written or recorded sources. In general parlance, though, "folk music" in the nineteenth century stood for collectivity, communality and the rural. In America, mainstream music began to be more commodified in the early twentieth century, with the advent of printing and recording industries (epitomized by Tin Pan Alley and the Brill Building). Folksong enthusiasts such as Cecil Sharp (1859–1924), John A. Lomax (1867–1948) and Phillips Barry (1880–1937) began collecting field recordings of the music, establishing early libraries of American folk music.

In the 1940s, social and economic factors led to a folk music revival in America and a development in character of the style. Many young people felt that the older generation had managed the world poorly, and voiced their opinions through song. Singers such as Woody Guthrie (1912–1967) and Pete Seeger (1919–2014) gained popularity, and the folk revival became associated with political stances such as anti-war and nuclear disarmament.[4] Alongside his musical activities, Seeger was also a music archeologist, researching and building a documentation of folk styles. Collector and ethnomusicologist Alan Lomax (1915–2002) built on and extended this new scholarly field, by collecting field recordings and building libraries of folk and world musics. The scholarly and the musical proceeded hand in hand, as folk musicians' dedication to writing from the heart was intertwined with preserving music from the past.

By the 1960s, the associations of folk music with radical politics and subversion began to fuse with the beatnik scene. The rise of the singer-songwriter in the mid-1960s led to songs by individual performers that were often personal, autobiographical and direct (perhaps the most well-known example is Bob Dylan). A general shift in folk singers' focus from singing about communities and collectivity ("we") to personal experience ("I") can be seen in Loudon's output in particular. Acoustic guitar accompaniment and an unmediated, open, singing style formed the basis of this late-1960s folk style – a movement embraced by both Kate and Loudon.[5]

Loudon and Kate's musical careers and lives intersected in the late-1960s New York folk scene. They were both active as part of the coffeehouse circuit in and around Greenwich Village, and met after Kate heard Loudon play at the Village Gaslight. A shared love of music and the honest and confessional folk style, as well as mutual respect for each other's musical creativity and careers, led to the beginning of one of the most renowned relationships in folk history.[6] The pair married in 1971 after learning that Kate was pregnant, ostensibly to avoid potential visa problems due to Kate's Canadian nationality. Their marriage anchored a tempestuous, but ultimately short-lived relationship. (Loudon and Kate divorced in 1976.) Their first joint venture was a lengthy European trip, where they visited Scandinavia and the Netherlands, before a large-scale argument resulted in them travelling on to England separately. Upon arrival in London, Loudon realized that *Album II* had been released there as well as in America, and persuaded his record company to organize an ad-hoc promotional London performance. (The pregnancy ended in a miscarriage, and the couple returned to New York, arguing and saddened.)

Alongside the developments in Kate's personal life, Kate and Anna continued their folk-music partnership at a distance throughout the late 1960s and early 1970s, although Kate's New York location meant that she was the first to be noticed by the music establishment. Folk singer Maria Muldaur recorded Kate's composition 'The Work Song' on her self-titled album (Reprise, 1973). Muldaur's producer Joe Boyd wanted to hear more of Kate's musical style and harmonies, and invited her to Los Angeles to produce a demo recording. Kate took Anna to sing with her at that appointment, and "it was in the Los Angeles demo studio that they became 'Kate and Anna McGarrigle'" (Lake, 2009: 24). Lenny Waronker, a key figure in Warner Brothers records and Boyd's co-producer on *Maria Muldaur*, offered Kate and Anna a recording contract in May 1974 after hearing their demo – and thus began the McGarrigle sisters' long recording career.

Rufus McGarrigle Wainwright was born in New York on 22 July 1973. By this point, Loudon was signed to Columbia Records, and in the year of Rufus's birth released two further albums, *Album III* and *Attempted Mustache*. Kate contributes vocals and banjo to *Attempted Mustache*, and in 'Dilated to Meet You', the couple explicitly address their anxieties about becoming parents. Lyrics such as "We're hoping you won't hurt too much/That you'll be alright" have a double meaning: expressing care for their first born, while also showing that Kate and Loudon were fearful of the pain their child may cause, both in labour and later. 'Lullaby', from the same album, specifically addresses Loudon's cares and concerns for the new child. Lines such as: "Shut up and go to bed ... I'm sick and tired of your worries", and "Shut your mouth and button your lips/You're a late-night faucet that's got a drip" contain a double meaning – they could just as easily be applied to Loudon in the third person as to the infant Rufus. These early songs are, however, well meaning and show a generosity of spirit on Loudon's part. Two years later, the song 'Rufus is a Tit Man' (on the 1975 album *Unrequited*) tells a different story. On the face of it, the song is a humorous reflection on Kate's nursing of Rufus. Reading between the lines, however, an underlying jealousy of Rufus's dominance of Kate's emotional and bodily attentions is evident. "Oh son, you look so satisfied, I envy you".

Loudon was not the only member of the family to express his emotions through song. *Kate and Anna McGarrigle* was released by Warner Brothers in 1975, and included the song 'Go Leave', in which Kate addresses Loudon, recalling the "times we used to laugh a lot", but ultimately asks him to leave her and their relationship. Their second album, *Dancer with Bruised Knees* (1977) included the joyful 'First Born', a song addressed to Rufus.

'First Born' opens with a sparse piano backdrop to a jubilant, gospel-inflected melody. The song features two contrasting verse melodies and a bridge. As the song progresses, instruments are added: bass, percussion, accordion and backing vocals add to the texture. Kate's love for Rufus and her unbounded joy at becoming a mother are apparent in the lyrics ("He's his mother's favourite ... No matter what comes next/Be it another boy or a sweet baby girl").

Much less positivity is conjured by Anna's song on the same album, 'Kitty Come Home'. Over a simple piano broken chordal backdrop, Anna beseeches her sister to "Pack up all your children/[and] Come home to your love and concern". Again, the musical accompaniment expands as the song progresses, with the addition of organ, recorder, and more voices.

Loudon had previously expressed his feelings in song about Kate's burgeoning musical career. A response to a review of one of Kate and Anna's live shows, 'Saw Your Name in the Paper' (*Album II*, 1971), made his jealousy clear. The song featured the opening lyrics: "It was quite a blow ... They said you stole the show". A desire for fame and fortune, and an inability to be unreservedly happy about his family's success, was to plague Loudon for life. In order to increase his time in the spotlight, he continually put himself forward for acting work, on top of his established musical career.[7] His 1983 album title *Fame and Wealth* underscores his ambitions.

Martha Wainwright was born in New York City on 8 May 1976. *Kate and Anna McGarrigle* was still doing well commercially, and had gained a following in the UK. The sisters toured England in the summer following Martha's birth, performing at folk festivals in smaller cities as well as venues in London. Loudon was also touring England at this time, and the fact that the couple did not travel or stay together is representative of the tension in their relationship that would lead to their divorce. Shortly after her return to the United States, Kate listened to Anna's advice in 'Kitty Come Home', and moved back to Montreal with her young children. Anna had married the Canadian journalist Dane Lanken in 1977 and had two children of her own, Sylvan (b. 1977) and Lily (b. 1979). Continuing the family tradition of musical collaboration, Dane provided backing vocals for *Kate and Anna McGarrigle* and *Dancer with Bruised Knees*. In stark contrast to Loudon's ambitions, Kate and Anna wished to retreat from the record industry and bring up their families in peace.

Kate and the children settled in a dilapidated Victorian house in the upmarket Westmount district of the city. Music was a common feature of family life, as the sisters rehearsed and developed their own repertoire around the house, and musical friends and acquaintances frequently visited. The children were always encouraged to sing with their mother and aunt, and to play the piano and various instruments in the house. Rufus began playing the piano aged six, and made his stage debut with Kate and Anna the same year. Both Rufus and Martha toured with the show seven years later.

Martha recalled the eclectic musical environment of the house, with young Rufus listening to Kate's Edith Piaf records, listening to classical music with Kate, and to the chart radio stations with Martha. The siblings' early nighttime routine betrays a sign of musical competition to come. Martha reminisced:

> Our rooms were at the end of a hallway ... and we'd sleep with the door open ... Starting when I was around seven and he was ten ... We would sing ourselves to sleep. Yelling, as loudly as we could. I remember Michael Jackson, or Cyndi Lauper, or Eurythmics, things that we had heard on the radio. But I, being the youngest, probably fell asleep first. So he yelled me into sleep. (Scott, 2009: 22:52)

Loudon had a number of romantic partners in the period that followed. Shortly after divorcing Kate, he moved the young folk singer Suzzy Roche into their New York apartment. His 1978 album *Final Exam* includes the song 'Pretty Little Martha', in which he explained that he missed Martha and Rufus, and would visit them often. In 1981, Suzzy gave birth to Lucy Wainwright Roche, to whom Suzzy's collaborative song with Loudon 'Screaming Issue' was dedicated. The song was featured on Loudon's 1986 album *I'm Alright*. The album also included 'Your Mother and I', a later song addressed to Lucy, explaining that Suzzy and he were splitting up, but that he would visit "on weekends, Christmas and the summer time too". Meanwhile, Kate entered a long-term relationship with bassist Pat Donaldson, who moved into the house in Westchester. Donaldson featured on several of the ensuing McGarrigle albums.[8]

A number of significant events occurred during Rufus's teenage years. Among these are such formative moments as coming out to his parents, both of whom initially responded negatively in different ways;[9] developing a passion for opera; and attending the private boarding school Millbrook in upstate New York, five hours drive away from the family's Montreal home. Many stories of Rufus's childhood have been cemented into mythology through repetition in various journalistic forms.[10] He, Martha and Kate repeat the same anecdotes frequently in media interviews, and the documentaries *All I Want* (Scott, 2005) and *Prima Donna: The Story of an Opera* (Scott, 2009) feature the same home videos.

One such repeated story is the entanglement of Rufus's growing awareness of his homosexuality with his discovery of the operatic idiom. Rufus stated: "I knew when I was very young, when I was about fourteen, that I was gay" (Scott, 2009: 10:08). Kate brought home a recording of Verdi's *Requiem* at around the same time, and Rufus immediately responded to the drama and excess of the musical style and characters evoked. Indeed, in a 2005 interview with the *New York Times*, he claimed that "opera saved my life twice" (Tommasini, 2005). According to Wainwright, opera first saved his life by providing an escape from the isolation and confusion he felt as a teenage homosexual – issues which will be considered in more depth in Chapter 3. The second life-saving period referred to his rehabilitation after drug misuse in the early 2000s.

The conflict between Rufus's growing talent for folk-influenced popular songwriting and his passion for opera and art music is evidenced in his recollections of becoming an opera fan. After discovering Verdi, Rufus would explore his mother's record collection for obscure opera to listen to, as well as bringing home records from school. His tastes diverged from Martha's, who preferred to listen to the charting hits on the radio. Fearing that he would be ostracized by his peers, Kate encouraged him to listen to the popular music of the day – but he dismissed this as "poor people's music" (Lake, 2009: 52).

As a teenager, Rufus often convinced Martha and his cousins to act out modern-day settings of operas with him, to be captured on home videos. While Rufus was attending Millbrook, Kate and Anna were invited to contribute a soundtrack for a 1988 Canadian children's film, *Tommy Tricker and the Stamp Traveller* (dir. Mike Rubbo). The film is an imaginative juvenile adventure – the premise is that the protagonist Tommy discovers that it is possible to shrink himself onto postage stamps, and thus travel the world by airmail. Kate and Anna contributed an instrumental soundtrack, and when Rubbo decided he wanted to incorporate a song, they suggested that he utilize Rufus's growing songwriting talents. The resulting blues and rock inflected 'I'm a-Runnin'' greatly impressed Rubbo, and he engineered a plot device that enabled Rufus to perform the song in the film.[11] In keeping with the Wainwright/McGarrigle tradition of working as a family, Martha sang 'Tommy Come Home' over the end credits. Rubbo's film script and Rufus's song were nominated for Genies (the Canadian Film Academy's annual award), bringing Rufus and his music to public prominence.

Rufus continued writing his own songs, and soon built up a substantial original repertoire. After graduating from Millbrook in 1991, Rufus began studying classical piano at McGill University in Montreal. Shortly afterwards, he dropped out. He returned to the family home and began performing in local nightclubs and coffee shops, and often invited Martha to sing backup for him, or perform a song or two of her own.

Sharing performance opportunities remained a constant in the Wainwright family. Despite his emotional distance from his children and former wife, Loudon remained visible in their lives. Loudon was so impressed by one of Rufus's early performances that he offered him an opening slot in his forthcoming tour the following year. After a few nervous early performances, Rufus began to receive as much – if not more – encouragement from the audiences than Loudon. What had initially begun as a generous gesture from father to son became another point of friction in their relationship. Their competing levels of fame, and their conflicting relationships, are explored later in this chapter regarding Rufus's song 'Dinner at Eight'.

Soon afterwards, Rufus fell in love with a straight man named Danny. Using the inspiration of his nascent emotions, and building on his family's connections in the music business, he recorded a demo cassette with producer Pierre Marchand, who had recently recorded *Heartbeats Accelerating* (1990) for Kate and Anna, and would soon record *Matapédia* (1995). Marchand is an acclaimed songwriter, musician and record producer, who since

1991 was well-known for his production work with singer-songwriter Sarah McLachlan. Marchand later developed a sustained working relationship with Rufus Wainwright.

The privately produced cassette (now known as *Rufus Wainwright/Songs*) contained the songs 'Foolish Love'; 'Heart Like a Highway'; 'Money Song'; 'Danny Boy'; 'Beauty Mark'; 'Damned Ladies'; 'Liberty Cabbage'; 'Ashes' and 'Matinee Idol'. Rufus moved to New York City with his demo tape, in pursuit of stardom and a musical career. He was part of a surge of singer-songwriters seeking success in New York (among whom number Jeff Buckley, Ben Folds and David Gray), and did not receive a response to his tape. Disillusioned by what he perceived as a personal rejection, and disheartened from working a series of odd jobs to make ends meet, he returned once again to the family house in Montreal.

Rufus was still determined to pursue a career in music, and to get his songs heard. From the security of the family home, he began playing at any available venue, often for next to no payment. He soon gained a residency at Café Sarajevo on Clark Street in Montreal. At the time, Café Sarajevo was a small, intimate live music venue that often featured blues, jazz and gypsy music. The eclecticism of styles favoured by owner Osman Koulenovitch demonstrated an open-mindedness that would allow Rufus's songs with their many musical influences to flourish.[12] It is here that he developed his performance style and rapport with the audience. With regular performances from October 1994, Rufus Wainwright (with backing vocals and the occasional solo spot provided by Martha) began to draw large crowds to this small coffeehouse venue.

Loudon's connections soon proved of value again. Some members of the audience at Rufus's gigs had compared his eclectic musical style with that of Van Dyke Parks and Randy Newman. Van Dyke Parks had a vast breadth of musical experience, and of nurturing others' musical talent (such as Harry Nilsson and the Beach Boys) through collaboration and production. His own 1968 solo album *Song Cycle* is eclectic, drawing from contemporary idioms such as folk and baroque pop, as well as older styles such as ragtime and Dixieland. Instruments on the record range from synthesizer to orchestral brass and strings. *Song Cycle* had been produced at high cost by Waronker and released by Warner Bros Records, who made a financial loss, but the record gained a cult following. (Waronker and Parks's collaboration on *Song Cycle* established a pattern of production, marketing and consumption that was to be repeated several times with Rufus.) Remembering that Loudon had a previous acquaintance with Parks, Rufus asked him to pass on a demo cassette. Loudon duly did so, and an impressed Parks passed it on to Lenny Waronker, who had recently left Warner to run the newly founded DreamWorks Records with Mo Ostin. Waronker invited Rufus to fly to Los Angeles to meet him, and offered him a contract with the company shortly after. Again, family connections were useful to Rufus – as mentioned earlier, Waronker offered Kate and Anna their initial contract with Warner Bros in 1974.

Continuing in the Wainwright/McGarrigle tradition, Rufus expressed his relationships with other members of his family through original song. In each case, his characteristic style is influenced by different genres: 'Beauty Mark', for Kate, bears genre markings of ragtime and musical theatre; 'Little Sister', obliquely about Martha, is a classical pastiche; and 'Dinner at Eight', to Loudon, is a more stereotypical rock song.[13]

Neil Tennant (of the English electro-pop duo the Pet Shop Boys, and producer of 2007's *Release the Stars*) commented on Rufus's musical influences, suggesting that they can be directly related to his family, upbringing and experiences:

> Rufus I really like, because I also like classical music, I like theatre music, and I can tell Rufus was very much influenced by the classical thing, by what you might call show tunes ... by American songwriting of the pre-rock era, like Stephen Foster and stuff like that ... I guess that because of his mother and family you've also got the folk thing going. So it's a very interesting selection of influences. And yet at the same time, this is someone who had stood in gay bars and had pounding Eurodisco playing. (Scott, 2005: 1:00:52)

American singer-songwriter and family friend Cherry Vanilla commented in 2009 on Rufus's relationship with Kate: "His mother's the closest person to him in his whole life. It's mother and son on one hand, and best friends on the other" (Scott, 2009: 1:02:00). Many aspects of this relationship are encapsulated by Rufus's early song 'Beauty Mark'.

'Beauty Mark' was one of the demo tracks he produced in 1995 with Pierre Marchand, and was later officially released on *Rufus Wainwright*. The short (2:14) song is stylistically upbeat, beginning with a rolling piano figure ("neo-Honky Tonk", as Kate described it [Scott, 2009: 41:20]), accented by timpani and glockenspiel. The song is in simple verse form, with three verses alternating with contrasting refrains. Rufus sings a melodic rubato over the rhythmic and harmonic underpinning: here, this creates an air of joyfulness and urgency, as though he is rushing ahead to proclaim his feelings for his mother and to embrace his burgeoning career.

'Beauty Mark'

Kevin C. Schwandt describes 'Beauty Mark' as Rufus's "love song to his mother" (2010: 85) – and, indeed, Wainwright's life and career decisions reflect this adoration of Kate. He has spoken in numerous interviews about his affection and respect for his mother, has appeared in many of her live performances and records, and their tactile and loving relationship is a frequent feature of Rufus's DVD documentaries. In a trait that was to become a feature of Wainwright's output, the song engages with biographical background, and it also offers a veiled comment on his awareness and growing acceptance of his own sexuality while also offering a commentary on his relationship with his mother.

In verses 1 and 2, Wainwright sings about the physical and emotional characteristics that he does not share with Kate. "I never had your beauty mark ... your black hair and hazel eyes ... a fear of nuns who dressed in black". In the refrains, he sings about the traits he *did* inherit: "But I do have your taste ... round face and long hands". Wainwright pauses on each of the inherited characteristics.

Many things are encapsulated with the lyrics of the final verse:

Table 1.1: 'Beauty Mark', verse 3

I think Callas sang a lovely Norma
You prefer Robeson on 'Deep River'
I may not be so manly
But I know you still love me

By referring to Maria Callas as his vocal idol, he connects to the phenomenon of gay adoration of opera divas explored by Wayne Koestenbaum in *The Queen's Throat* – an issue discussed further in Chapter 3. These lyrics reinforce Kate's place in the folk music tradition, and the different musical tastes she and Rufus enjoyed. The verse also alludes to the vocal differences between Robeson's traditionally masculine basso profundo, and Rufus's capacity for a high vocal register and operatic tendencies, alluding to the initial difficulties that she and Loudon had in accepting Rufus's homosexuality.

Kate was diagnosed with the rare cancer sarcoma about the time Rufus gained the commission for the opera. While based in Berlin in 2007 to record *Release the Stars*, Rufus began a relationship with Jörn Weisbrodt, who at the time was Head of Special Projects at the Berlin Opera. Rufus went on to "co-parent" a daughter with Jörn (Viva Wainwright was born to Leonard Cohen's daughter Lorca on 2 February 2011), and the couple married on 24 August 2012. Jörn emphasized the circularity of Kate's importance to the opera project: "Kate's illness has kept him going with the work, and then also the work was always communicated back to Kate, and that sort of kept her going" (Scott, 2009: 1:05:00).

Rufus documented this period in 'Zebulon', released on the 2010 album *All Days are Nights: Songs for Lulu*, singing: "My mother's at the hospital/my sister's at the opera". Kate died of her illness in January 2010. The Wainwright siblings and friends/musical collaborators appeared at a Celebration of Kate McGarrigle concert at the Meltdown Festival at London's Southbank, on 12 June 2010. Further commemorative concerts were held at New York City Town Hall on 12–13 May 2011, and in November 2012 the concert movie *Sing Me The Songs That Say I Love You: A Concert for Kate McGarrigle* was released (dir. Liam Lunson, 2012). This was followed in summer 2013 by a double CD compilation album of selected songs from the concerts (produced by Joe Boyd).

Martha

Rufus's relationship with his sister Martha was very close throughout their childhood, and remains so at the time of writing. They shared a musical upbringing, involving singing with their mother and aunt – and at times, their father – "yelling" each other to sleep, and acting out operas as childhood games.

Martha spent a troubled year with Loudon in New York at the age of fifteen, in an attempt to develop their relationship. The year was not a success emotionally. Musically, however, Loudon significantly furthered Martha's development, by buying her a guitar and providing her with fodder for autobiographical songs. Her first foray into songwriting was 'The Lexie Song', written about the daughter Loudon had with a new girlfriend, Ritamarie Kelly. When she returned to Montreal the year after, she began to sing with Rufus at his local gigs. Martha produced her first album independently; a cassette entitled *Ground Floor* (1997). Although initially supportive of her career, and keen to include her in his own music-making efforts, Rufus's capacity to compete and provoke came to the fore in 'Little Sister' (produced by Marchand for the 1995 demo, although not released until 2004's *Want Two*).

'Little Sister'

'Little Sister' is voiced in a typically Mozartian fashion, with a string orchestra in homophonic motion (where all parts are in rhythmic unison, with the harmonic relationship between them creating shifting chords), a harpsichord and a piano to the fore of the instrumental accompaniment. The lyrical content serves a double meaning, referring to two famous musical sibling relationships: Wolfgang and Maria Anna Mozart, and Rufus and Martha Wainwright. Opportunities did not favour eighteenth-century female musicians, and it was Wolfgang who gained notoriety and a place in history as a musician and composer. Although ostensibly a monologue from Wolfgang to Maria Anna, the parallels with Rufus and Martha are direct enough to assume that this is intended as a contemporary commentary. Through the allegory created by the song, Rufus is able to subtly tease his sister about her musical career: "History is on my side ... Remember that your brother is a boy". (As a side note, Rufus and Martha often appear together in concert, and often share interview spreads in newspapers and magazines. They always appear to get along very well, and so 'Little Sister' can be assumed to be playful.)

The song contains two verses, each with a refrain. A Mozartian pastiche short string figure introduces the song, separates the verses, appears again before a rubato coda, and closes the song. Rufus begins by acknowledging their shared musical upbringing, and alludes to their similar careers in music: "Little sister come and sit beside me/And we'll play a tune on the piano". Again continuing the allegorical comparison with the eighteenth-century pair of siblings, and acknowledging the gender hierarchy of centuries earlier in which women were expected to be a muted and decorative asset to their husbands, he suggests that his sister will harmlessly play the piano "Til your hair becomes a powdered wig ... You may have to use your hips as fodder". The latter lyric has two potential meanings: as well as commenting on the inevitability of childbearing and rearing life for women, it perhaps unconsciously betrays an anxiety of childlessness he holds as a homosexual man. He returns to the idea of children to end the song.

In contrast, he as the favoured first-born male child has the freedom to "become a total bastard" as he pursues his musical dream. Nonetheless, Martha's/Maria Anna's "feet [are] sewn to a tremendous shadow", and the siblings are bound to go through life together. The lines "remember that round one has just been played" and "before we go round again" suggest that the imagined historical event is but a stopping point in a sequence of events that is destined to repeat.

Despite continuing to sing backing vocals for Rufus live and on record, Martha went on to have an independent recording career, releasing *Martha Wainwright* in 2005, *I Know You're Married But I've Got Feelings Too* in 2008 and *Come Home to Mama* in 2012. She married the bassist and backing vocalist on her first album, Brad Albetta, in 2007, and they had their first child, Arcangelo, in 2010. Lily Lanken, Rufus, Kate and Anna all provided backing vocals for the earlier two albums, and after Kate's death, Martha used her song 'Proserpina' on *Come Home to Mama*.

Nonetheless, the siblings' musical and personal relationship remained close enough that Martha frequently toured with Rufus, and appeared singing background vocals on all his albums, bar the piano and vocal solo album *All Days are Nights: Songs for Lulu* (2010). Rendered more powerful by her musical absence, 'Martha', the third song on *All Days are Nights*, is a direct appeal to his sister, beseeching her to help him put aside any differences and look after their parents. Rufus begins each verse with "Martha it's your brother calling", going on to proclaim that it is "time to go up north and see mother". In the second verse, he suggests that they put aside their differences with Loudon, asking: "Have you had a chance to see father?/Wondering how he's doing/ There's not much time for us to really be that angry at each other anymore". ('Martha' is analysed further in Chapter 5.)

Loudon

Despite his physical distance from Rufus and Martha, Loudon tried to remain an active parental presence. Nevertheless, Rufus's relationship with his father was troubled. Rufus felt abandoned as a child, and even went as far as pinning some of his early sexual explorations upon the need for a male role model in his life. He reflected upon his eager discovery of the gay bars of Montreal in his teens: "On the one hand it was sexual, but on the other hand it was perhaps a need for some kind of male figure in my life in general" (Scott, 2005: 10:43).

In a 2005 interview with British journalist Tim Adams, Rufus commented upon Loudon's tendency to address difficult relationships through song:

> He certainly dealt onstage I think more directly with the anatomy of his family than any other performer I know. He had a song for every family member, every situation. And my mother did the same thing in a way. At the same time, though, my father was very distant from us and very hard to get to at all. (Adams, 2005)

Both the Wainwright children felt increasingly uncomfortable with Loudon's tendency to play out his relationships in song. Eventually, Rufus responded in kind, writing the emotionally charged 'Dinner at Eight' (released on *Want One*). The song centres on a meeting between Rufus and Loudon, in which they discussed their respective levels of fame over dinner. Rufus suggested that Loudon's career was past its prime, and the only way he could feature in *Rolling Stone* at this stage of his life would be because he was Rufus's father.[14] Loudon's hunger for fame and notoriety had not abated by this point. Nor had Rufus's ego, nor his capacity to provoke those close to him. According to Rufus's interview with Adams, Loudon threatened to kill him after the comment.

'Dinner at Eight'

'Dinner at Eight' began as a documentation of this incident, and also draws upon biblical stories and age-old proverbs as allegories. It is deceptively simple in structure and in lyrics, but reveals complexities upon examination.

The song opens with a four-bar broken chordal piano figure in 4/4; a simple and unaffected musical device that underpins the entirety. It consists of four verses, with a contrasting interlude as a bridge between verses 3 and 4, before a repeat of verse 1. As is typical of Rufus Wainwright compositions, the clear structure that is first audible masks greater depths. Each verse begins with an anticipatory figure, followed by the same sixteen bars, which is then extended in each consecutive verse with the addition of lyric lines, rubato, cross-rhythms and pauses. In combination with mounting instrumental accompaniment (strings, French horns, woodwinds and harp are added over the course of the first three verses), this structure lends emotional weight to the lyrics, allowing the listener time to reflect on the meaning.

Table 1.2: 'Dinner at Eight', song structure

Instrumental introduction:	0:00
Verse 1:	0:09
Verse 2:	0:35
Verse 3:	1:15
Bridge:	2:10
Verse 4:	2:58
Verse 1 repeat:	3:50 (ends 4:31)

Conflating the biblical parable of David and Goliath with the nineteenth-century English rhyme "sticks and stones may break my bones, but words will never hurt me", in verse 1, Rufus threatens to "take [Loudon] down with one little stone". By bringing together the two images, Rufus suggests that he is aware that Loudon will be hurt by his words, and that he knows exactly which angle to take to be the most hurtful. However, Rufus follows this with a lyrical twist clearly influenced by Loudon's autobiographical narrative decades earlier in 'Lullaby', turning the attack on himself. The outcome of breaking Loudon's spirit with the metaphorical stone will be to "see what you're worth to me".

Verse 2 begins with the lyric that gives the song its title. 'Dinner at Eight' not only refers to the meeting at which the verbal battle in question took place, but alludes to George Cukor's 1933 film of the same name. The comic melodrama focuses on a chaotic society dinner hosted by Millicent Jordan (a character played by Billie Burke). Burke would go on to play Glinda in the 1939 film version of *The Wizard of Oz*, which could suggest that the song's title was relevant to Rufus's sexual identity as well as his relationship with his father. Wainwright reflects precisely upon the incident that reignited old conflicts with Loudon, singing about the "toasts full of gleams" and the "old magazines

[that] got us started up again". His choice of words is apt, for not only do the syllables scan exactly to mirror verse 1, but to "gleam" means to shine brightly with a light reflected from another source. Rufus's lyric choice captures Loudon's envy and frustration, while remaining understated. Yet, by the end of the verse, he again turns to self-doubt, blaming himself rather than the magazines for provoking his father's fury. "Actually, it was probably me again", he sings. This final line of the verse extends the form, with expressive rubato as he deliberates over the lyrics. Rufus delays over the three syllables of "actually" and "probably", giving further pause for reflection. At this point, French horns and strings play ascending figures, underscoring the Romanticism suggested by his tempo fluctuations with textures from the same era.[15]

In verse 3, Rufus contemplates the nature of his separation from his father. In a series of rhetorical questions, he asks why he – the son – feels compelled to leave their arguments. He turns the narrative back to Loudon, explaining that "you were the one/Long ago, actually in the drifting white snow/Who left me". The verse form is again extended, and the delayed vocal melodies are heard again on the three-syllable groupings of "actually" and "drifting white". Rufus's description of the snow evokes his childhood in Montreal, as well as winters in Manhattan. It is also a general symbol of desolation and loneliness, expressing his feelings towards Loudon. A pause on the final line again allows reflection, after which a harp arpeggio is heard alongside a descending flute figure.

The orchestral backing swells to support the contrasting melody of the bridge. The vocal melody is higher in pitch than the previous verses, and features a repeated high note, which Rufus sings louder. This is the dramatic climax of the song, suggesting an imagined future site of resolution to the life-long battle: "Somewhere near the end of the world/Somewhere near the end of our lives". The instrumental accompaniment fades out, so that just the continuing piano figure can be heard. Moderating his vocal delivery, Rufus sings:

Table 1.3: 'Dinner at Eight', verse 4

But till then no daddy don't be surprised
If I want to see the tears in your eyes
Then I know it had to be, long ago
Actually, in the drifting white snow
You loved me.

French horn and strings re-enter for the final two lines, playing soft descending figures before the delay on "actually" and "drifting white". The form is extended further as Rufus holds the final line over descending woodwind figures. The song closes with a contemplative repeat of verse 1. The range of emotions lyrically and musically in 'Dinner at Eight' is vast, leading Kirk Lake to deem it Rufus's "love/hate song to Loudon" (2009: 183).

'Want'

Rufus's growing understanding of family life and contentment with his place in his own family is expressed in the song 'Want', which is featured on *Want One* – and from which the *Want* albums take their name. The song consists of three sixteen-bar AABB verses, with Romantic rubato (tempo fluctuation) within each of the four-bar vocal lines. Verses 2 and 3 are followed with a refrain and instrumental outro.

The use of the term "want" is ambiguous, meaning both to need and to desire. In verse 1, Rufus sings a series of balanced statements, presenting first a negative and then a positive want: for example "I don't want to make it rain/I just want to keep it simple". He ends the first verse by suggesting that he wishes to strike out on his own musically, stating that he does not want to be "John Lennon or Leonard Cohen".

Verse 2 contains the most interesting lyrical content for this discussion of the Wainwright family:

Table 1.4: 'Want', verse 2

I just want to be my Dad
With a slight sprinkling of my mother
And work at the family store
And take orders from the counter

A sense of contentment (or perhaps resignation) with his place in his own family can be noted here. Loudon expressed similar emotions in 'A Father and A Son' (released on *History* in 1992), where he explained the cyclical nature of filial relationships, documenting past arguments and powers struggles between himself and his own father before the eventual realization that the adult Loudon resembled his father, and was going through the same issues with Rufus. "Maybe it's hate/but probably it's love" sings Loudon.

Placed two songs earlier than the poignant 'Dinner at Eight', in 'Want' Rufus seems to acknowledge the inevitability – and the desirability – of taking after his parents. Working at the family store can be read as a mundane analogy for following in his parents' career choices and becoming a performing musician. In a rare exception to the lack of specific references in his pop songs, he contextually places 'Want' by going on to state that he does not want to be John Lithgow or Jane Curtin – both actors in the sitcom *Third Rock From the*

Sun, which ran from 1996–2001. The music slows to a pause on "Jane Curtin", and echo is placed on Rufus's voice.

The refrain that follows verse 2 begins with an out-of-time pick-up "But I'll", before resuming the initial tempo and implying that all his wants can be solved by "settl[ing] for love". Verse 3 is the musical climax of the song, as backing vocals are added to the texture. As usual, Martha provides one of the additional vocal lines, while Jenni Muldaur sings the other. (Jenni is the daughter of Maria Muldaur, who inadvertently provided Kate's first break-through in the musical world.) Lyrically, the verse addresses movement and stasis. "Before I reached the gate/I realized I had packed my passport", Rufus sings. This could be an indirect allusion to his subsequent addiction to drugs and alcohol. According to Lake, 'Want' was written on his last day in rehabili-tation, and represented both contentment with his place in life and a desire to get back to work (2009: 183). The lyric metaphorically suggests that he real-ized he did not need to search elsewhere for fulfilment, and that the family and life he had been born into would suffice. By packing his passport, he – perhaps intentionally – ensures that he stayed.

Wainwright again demonstrated his contentment within his immediate and extended family during what was arguably his most notorious concert series to date. He performed a five-night residency at London's Royal Opera House in Covent Garden, on 18–23 July 2011. He performed a range of mate-rial during the week, including material from his tribute to Judy Garland on 18 and 21 July, performances with Martha and Loudon on 19 and 21 July, and concert performances from *Prima Donna*, featuring Janis Kelly and Rebecca Bottone playing older and younger versions of the title role, and the Britten Sinfonia conducted by Stephen Oremus.

Theories abound in journalism and Wainwright's online fan forum as to why the week was dubbed "House of Rufus". The most obvious explanation is a play on the famous Royal Opera House name. Much of the advertising for the venue contains the tagline "Velvet, Gilt and Glamour", alluding to the grandeur and opulence of the building and the productions that take place within.[16] Rufus's management adapted this phrase for his residency, adver-tising the subtly different "five nights of velvet, glamour and guilt" – render-ing the phrase a tongue-in-cheek slant on Rufus's lifestyle and flamboyance. Rufus was not immune to the cultural status of the venue, which helped him realize some of his operatic ambitions and dreams. After the final perfor-mance of *Prima Donna*, Rufus gleefully exclaimed to the audience "I tricked you! I got my opera into the Royal Opera House!"

Rufus later released a nineteen-disc boxed set of his entire works under the same name. Bound in red velvet, the contents ranged from demo tapes and covers, to his studio-produced albums, to the DVD that accompanied *Prima*

Donna. He stated: "I originally wanted to call this set The Rufus Cycle, y'know, like the Ring Cycle. But they said that was too sophisticated, so I Gagaed down" (Troussé, 2011). A hierarchical attitude towards popular music (Gaga) as opposed to the highbrow idiom of opera (Wagner) is again apparent. A thread on the fan message board of Rufus Wainwright's official website offers another explanation for the name "House of Rufus". "Danielle2020" posted on 22 July 2011: "the house of rufus was about family. this is his true home [*sic*]." "ShadowWing" concurs, suggesting that:

> [The] House of Rufus might mean that he is giving his audience a rare, inside look at his *actual house*. How blessed you are because you are able to see the whole Wainwright family, finally together. Loudon and Lucy and Martha and Rufus and all on stage together performing.[17]

Many aspects of Rufus's life and musical output were represented during the final concert of the series. Extracts from his 2009 opera *Prima Donna* formed the first half. The second consisted of a selection of his existing hits, his family's songs, and art songs: 'Le Spectre de la Rose' (Berlioz); 'Vibrate'; 'Soave si il vento' (Mozart, from *Cosi fan Tutti*, sung with Janis Kelly and Rebecca Bottone); 'Last Rose of Summer' (traditional Irish); 'Kitty Come Home' (Anna McGarrigle); 'Oh What a World' (in which he changed a lyric from "always travelling but not in love" to "always travelling but still in love", reflecting his relationship status – by this point, he was engaged to Jörn); 'If I Loved You' (from *Carousel*, sung with Rebecca Bottone); and 'L'Absence' (Berlioz). Members of his family performed their own material, before coming together in a joint performance of 'Sweet Thames, Flow Softly', by Ewan MacColl, one of the leading figures in the English folk song revival of the 1950s. The peaceful, gentle song acknowledges the river that flows through the city, situating the performance in London. Beginning with Rufus, the family and friends alternate verses, joining together in the folk harmonies of the chorus. Martha sings the second verse, and Calum MacColl the third. Calum MacColl, a folk singer-songwriter and producer in England, is the son of Ewan MacColl and Peggy Seeger, another example of a musical family lineage.[18] Lily Lanken follows MacColl's verse, and Rufus sings the last verse. By ending his programme, and the House of Rufus, with 'Sweet Thames, Flow Softly', Rufus situates himself and his family even more firmly in folk history.

That night, Rufus Wainwright oversaw the performance of extracts from his opera in one of the most prestigious opera houses in the world. During the evening he paid tribute to his late mother, and called out lovingly to his fiancé and daughter. As the final number drew to a close, Rufus shared the stage and the vocal platform with his cousin Lily, his sister Martha, his brother-in-law Brad Albetta, special guest MacColl, and his father Loudon. Laughing and joking in between numbers, Rufus Wainwright appeared content with his lot.

2 Western Art Music and Pop: Conflict and Coherence

> He really harkens ... to that age of the singer-songwriter. He writes songs that are pop songs, pop songs with depth. I think there is – because of his influences, and because it ranges from classical music to pop, I just think there's so much to find in what he does. There's complexity there, but it's also just instantly accessible.
>
> (Babydaddy from Scissor Sisters, in *All I Want*, dir. Scott, 2005: 54:10)

> Pop music is my bread and butter.
>
> (Wainwright in Vaziri, 2012)

> Now I've ... conquered the opera world.
>
> (Wainwright in Swift, 2012)

Rufus Wainwright sits between two artistic worlds. He has made his name as a popular musician, with seven commercially successful studio albums at the time of writing, numerous contributions to and appearances in Hollywood films, and hundreds of live performances featuring a larger-than-life persona.[1] And yet, another artistic world has always been present in his life and music. As an isolated homosexual teenager in the mid-1980s, he found solace and comfort in the operas of Giuseppe Verdi. Musical and verbal references to Verdi's operas, and more generally, to western art music and the surrounding traditions, feature continually in his popular song and artistic ventures. For example, 'Damned Ladies' from his first album (*Rufus Wainwright*, Dream-Works, 1998) is addressed directly to eight operatic heroines. Although his pop songs can usually be placed into common pop and rock song structures, certain musical and verbal characteristics separate Rufus Wainwright's music from pop convention. In recent years, Wainwright has manifested his interest in the classical music world through a series of collaborations and works on the art music platform. This chapter explores the classical music persona that he has created, which exists alongside, and is sometimes integrated into, his existing popular music persona.

Allan Moore's explanation of the four functional layers of popular song provides a useful set of criteria with which to evaluate Wainwright's adherence to expected convention in pop and rock. Rather than a specific instrumentation, Moore comments, listeners expect four layers of sound: the *explicit beat layer* (consisting of some variety of percussion); the *functional bass layer* (whose pitch role is to connect root position harmonies); the *harmonic filler layer* (containing the greatest variety of instruments, from "rhythm guitars, organs and pianos to saxophone choirs, voices, brass sections, even entire orchestras"); and the *melodic layer* (containing the lead vocal, and often backing vocals and melody instruments supporting the primary line and supplying countermelodies) (Moore, 2012: 20–21). Wainwright's choice of instruments to construct the four functional layers is telling. Each album has a distinct sound world, supporting the oscillation between attracting a commercial audience and fulfilling large-scale artistic ideas. Each album (save the spartan *All Days are Nights*) features some variety of percussion, creating the "explicit beat layer". A range of acoustic and electric bass instruments fulfils the "functional bass layer" on his popular music output. Although he occasionally accompanies himself on guitar, his "harmonic filler" instrument of choice is the piano, which he uses to virtuosic effect.[2] Complex and numerous layers of orchestration and techniques typically associated with the classical music sound world also feature in the harmonic filler, as well as occasional soloistic moments in the melodic layer in *Rufus Wainwright*, *Want One/Two*, *Release the Stars* and *Out of the Game*. Wainwright's vocal forms the melodic layer, with increasing prominence throughout his recorded career (as explained further in Chapter 5).

Wainwright's views on music education suggest a dichotomy between popular music and western art music. Upon leaving school in 1991, he began studying music at McGill University in Canada. In interviews, he has repeatedly emphasized that he studied "classical" piano and composition – the genre is significant. Tellingly, he found the formal aspects of learning piano and compositional techniques restrictive. Comments by Rufus and his family illustrate the perceived dichotomy between art and popular music. Rufus recalled how his mother Kate McGarrigle had initially encouraged him to gain a formal music education, but later supported his decision to drop out after eighteen months, choosing to pursue his own songwriting and performance goals. Wainwright explained his stance on classical music education and personal identity in popular music:

> I don't regret not totally pursuing the classical agenda ... I will say in retrospect [that] I feel like I might have dodged a bullet there. In my opinion, a lot of people who come in through that heavy-duty conservatory system, they get indoctrinated, and definitely have to fit into some slot historically. And I don't have those boundaries that a lot of the classical musicians have. (Barber and O'Connor, 2014)

McGarrigle concludes that he "wasn't going to need the [conservatory/ university education], because he's going to be in the pop world" (Scott, 2009: 39:28). Wainwright concurred, stating that "you don't develop as a songwriter. You either are a songwriter or you're not. There's no way to learn it" (Scott, 2009: 9:40). This opinion can be understood from Wainwright's perspective as he entered higher education in 1991. However, as I write twenty-four years later, dozens of institutions around the world now offer songwriting courses at university level (Bennett, Shank and Toynbee, 2006: 5). Some of the routes through formal musical education taken by Wainwright's family, friends and mentors offer alternative perspectives on, support and challenges to the value of a formal musical education.

The term "western art music" covers a wide range of classical music and references, from the medieval to the present day. While the majority of Rufus Wainwright's non-popular musical techniques and lyrical references come from the later nineteenth-/early twentieth-century operatic repertoire, several come from other canons. 'The Art Teacher', for example (analysed in Chapter 4) uses a New York Philip Glass-like sound world. Many songs contain more references to Schubertian and Schumannian Lied than nineteenth-century opera, while the folk influences of his family as well as musical theatre can also be heard.

'Imaginary Love'

Associations with western art music are present in Rufus Wainwright's popular music output as early as his first album (1998). The closing song, 'Imaginary Love', contains the line "Schubert bust my brain". This line can be taken in several ways, suggesting the protagonist's mind being expanded by the Austrian composer Franz Schubert (1797–1828), a confusion caused by the technical compositional aspects of a formal musical education, or a connection between the contemporary singer-songwriter and the life and works of the nineteenth-century composer. Schubert made important contributions to western art music in the fields of orchestral music, chamber music, piano music and the Lied. "Lied" can be translated to mean "a song in the German vernacular", but is generally used to refer to the setting of German poetry for solo voice and piano, with narrative and dramatic direction created by the interplay between two musical voices, and between the small-scale and large-scale poetic and musical structure. Schubert left behind more than 630 Lied when he died, leading to the composer being affectionately dubbed "the father of the Lied" (Gibbs, 1997: 8).

'Imaginary Love' contains some musical and verbal allusions to Schubert, but is not a stylistic imitation. The song, featuring Rufus on piano and vocals,

Jim Keltner on drums, Glen Hollman on upright bass, and Jon Brion on guitar, background vocals and pick bass, explores a sound world that morphs from synthesized popular music to acoustic art song and back.

'Imaginary Love' uses a contrasting verse-chorus scheme, with verse material heard once in the middle of the song (Table 2.1 shows the formal structure). It begins with a warped and distorted piano sound, implying that the "imaginary love" of the song takes place in an unidentifiable – or fantasy – location. The synthesized sound world is also reflective of popular music, having been introduced in the 1950s, explored by 1960s groups such as the Beach Boys and the Beatles, various exponents of the 1960s–70s progressive rock idiom, and used to varying degrees since. This sound world is implied more strongly by the introduction of a surf guitar (electric guitar with "wet" spring reverb), a sound frequently employed by the Beach Boys. The drum feel is a simple 12/8 hi-hat accompaniment, evocative of a 1950s shuffle. After two beats, the synthesizer develops into an alternating quaver figure heard in both Keltner's rolling drum patterns and an unobtrusive acoustic piano part based on the underlying harmony (notated in the following examples). The steady tempo (at around 67 crotchets a minute) suggests both the click track common to recordings of pop songs, and the good timekeeping and musicianship of Wainwright's chosen musicians.

Table 2.1: 'Imaginary Love' song structure

Synthesized shimmer intro
Instrumental introduction (0:03)
Chorus (0:10)
Verse (1:10)
Chorus (2:06)
Vocalese outro (3:05)

The complexity of his verbal content is heightened by his performance style: his use of monosyllables and exploitation of internal melismas in vowels support his statement that "lyrics are more important to me than music" (Barber and O'Connor, 2014). 'Imaginary Love' begins with a sixteen-bar chorus, a feature common to many popular songs. Here, the chorus consists of an eight-bar phrase repeated twice. It opens in the home key of Db, and chord changes are diatonic and on the beat.

The first line spans a range of a third, implying that "my kind of love" is restrictive in contemporary society. The melody repeats in the second phrase, with an expansion to a range of a sixth at the end of the line. Wainwright's piano becomes more audible at this point in the song. The song builds in dynamically to this point, which is heightened by Wainwright's repeat of the text and melody of the chorus an octave higher. The vocal performance is thus given a declamatory quality that can be seen to reinforce the emotion in the lyrical content.

Wainwright's vocal segues forwards into the contrasting verse material (1:10). This begins and ends in a dominant harmony, before the chorus is repeated in the home key of Db. During the bridge, the musical content enters a more Schubertian acoustic sound world, as the piano becomes more audible than the synthesized piano, which transforms into synthesized string harmonies and countermelodies, heard with backing vocals enhancing the lead vocal line. Here the melody line expands in range, showing the depth of Wainwright's singing voice by descending to an Eb below middle C. The harmonies change more frequently, with several related chords and pivot notes reached through descending stepwise harmony incorporating sevenths and sustained chords. Diminished harmonies and pivot chords for implied modulations are a hallmark of Schubert's piano style, and Wainwright pays implicit musical homage here. 'Imaginary Love' bears similarities to Schubert's famous Lied from 1825, 'Ave Maria' from *Ellen's Gesang* (Figure 2.1). The upwards melodic leap of a fourth, followed by descending stepwise intervals, is mimicked in Wainwright's "Hoped to look at you" (Figure 2.2, bar 1) and "at least my kind of love" (Figure 2.2, bars 1–2). Compositional similarities can also be seen in the use of a rippling, triplet feel piano accompaniment.

Figure 2.1: Schubert, *Ellen's Gesang* (1825), bb. 1–2

The repeat of the chorus is heard at its original pitch, but here with a strong acoustic piano line as well as synthesized strings, bringing the two sound worlds of the song together. As at the opening of the song, Wainwright repeats the chorus text an octave higher, here with both acoustic piano and synthesized keyboard strings. The song ends with four bars of Wainwright singing vocalese over tonic and subdominant harmonies. The entire song is a musical arc, progressing from predominantly synthesized sounds to primarily acoustic sounds and Schubertian compositional techniques and back, mirrored by lyri-

cal material that sets up the fantasy world of "imaginary love" before describing a specific (yet imagined) encounter, and returning to imagination.

Figure 2.2: 'Imaginary Love', bb. 1–4

When he is specifically referring to Schubert, the sound of Wainwright's
piano comes to the fore, and he enters an acoustic soundscape that can be
aligned with the art music world. As his musical career progressed, he brought
his own piano playing more to the forefront of his recorded output, ensuring
it could be heard even in complex and multi-layered arrangements. At other
times, Wainwright strips the sound world right back to piano and vocals, as is
the case for 'Pretty Things', and as we later see in the album *All Days are Nights:
Songs for Lulu* (2010). 'Imaginary Love' is a case of surface references to the art
music world.

Songwriting Technique

'Imaginary Love' has complex and multi-layered lyrics, contained within four-
bar phrases. This suggests that the art music references – in lyrical content,
textural devices or rubato melody lines – can all be layered upon a standard
popular song structure.

A feature of Wainwright's oeuvre is an improvisatory melody line seem-
ingly floating over the top of a metronomic background, which is a musical
connection to the nineteenth-century art music technique of rubato.[3] The
predominance of the piano in his accompaniments, and of the virtuosity of
the piano writing, further connects him to the performer-composer figures of
the nineteenth-century art music tradition – especially such famous figures as

Frédéric Chopin and Franz Liszt, who used these techniques. Wainwright uses rubato on two levels: first, by dragging the vocal line over a regular pulse in the instrumental accompaniment; and second, by slowing or accelerating the speed of the entire musical content. As a general rule, he slows or pauses on lyrics that encourage contemplation.

Wainwright is secretive about his songwriting process, choosing to keep his cards close to his chest until an entire song is worked out. An interviewer for the online magazine *Cool Cleveland* asked Wainwright about his creative process, and specifically whether he tends to write music or lyrics first. He replied:

> It's easier to do one first and then the other. The best music is written when you're not actively chasing it, but lyrics are a lot harder, I personally have to really hammer it out. The two processes require different parts of the brain, but it's great if it does happen simultaneously. (Nemeth, n.d.)

He later confirmed: "I'd say the melody and the chord structure come pretty quickly ... The lyrics are the bitch. So I have to play with those a little more" (Barber and O'Connor, 2014).

A BBC documentary aired in 2011 gives further insight into his compositional process. *Secrets of the Pop Song: Ballad* showed Wainwright collaborating with acclaimed British songwriter Guy Chambers to write a ballad in just two days of working time, alongside interviews with acclaimed and successful pop songwriters on the mechanics of success.[4] Critics and followers tend to seize upon a potential disadvantage in his musical upbringing from either popular music or the western art tradition, in order to make his achievements appear more impressive. This is demonstrated by the BBC narrator's concise summary of Wainwright's career to date, which presents him more as a classical musician than a popular music artist:

> Rufus has a massive following. His albums are a critical triumph. He's even written his own opera. This summer, he'll be the first ever contemporary artist to take up residency at the Royal Opera House. But can Rufus find success in the pop market? (*Secrets of the Pop Song*, 2:55)

The documentary begins with a day of collaboration at Chambers's recording studio in North London. Both artists bring preliminary material to the session: Chambers arrives with a suggested title, and Wainwright some rough sketches of musical material recorded on his Blackberry. Wainwright's musical ideas are promptly rejected, but he adopts Chambers's suggested title of 'World War III', and is taken with the lyrical themes implied – simultaneously applying the metaphors of warfare to political global battles, fights inside a family, and personal conflict between two characters. The documentary depicts Wainwright trying out lyrical and melodic figures over a piano riff brought to the session by Chambers. The impression conveyed is that Wainwright was able to achieve an almost fully formed melody and lyric, while Chambers provided a musical backdrop that he had worked on previously. The only stumbling block the pair is shown to face is when they cannot find a rhyme for the word "battle", and turn to a rhyming dictionary. It is unusual to see Wainwright involved in the mechanics of writing a song intended for the charts, because many of the interviews he gives maintain the idea that as an artist, he is struck by divine inspiration and conceives songs in their entirety (a common myth promoted by popular musicians' marketing teams, as explained by Joe Bennett in 2013). Wainwright's working methods here illustrate yet another parallel with Schubert's music and working methods. As Susan Youens explains: "Lieder begins with words; they are born when a composer encounters poetry" (in Gibbs, ed. 1997: 99). In the *Secrets of the Pop Song* documentary, we see Wainwright set an almost complete complex lyric to music, in a working process that mirrors Schubert's musical settings of existing poems.

The documentary also explores the personal nature of successful songs, suggesting that the main themes of commercially viable songs are love and loss. Allan Moore suggests one possible subject position for a rock singer, that of: "unrequited approaches, [and] love lost" (2001: 3). Many popular songs refer to these themes. Songwriter Sheila Davis states:

> Songs embody experiences common to everyone: the adventure of first love, the frustration of misunderstanding, the anguish of jealousy, the wistfulness of goodbye. A singer does not offer a sermon we must heed, or a code we must decipher, but rather a universal truth we already know. (1985: 3)

At the time of filming the first working day, Lorca Cohen was in the final weeks of pregnancy before giving birth to Wainwright's daughter, and he is open and confessional about the emotions and egos involved. Chambers comments that such openness is common amongst successful songwriters. This suggests the song will prompt what Allan Moore refers to as "second person authenticity" in which a listener's life experiences are validated by hearing them expressed through song (2002: 220).

Wainwright and Chambers meet for their second day of work a few months later, in Rufus's (then) hometown of Los Angeles. In the intervening months, Wainwright has become a father, and talks freely about the challenges and rewards he is facing. Wainwright's initial concern is with incorporating a quotation from Tchaikovsky's 1812 Overture, to underscore the military theme of the song. Throughout the course of the day, Wainwright overlays many vocal backing harmonies and double tracks, showing that his input on this second work day is largely melodic and lyrical rather than harmonic. (The mediation of the television producers' editing implies that Wainwright is rarely troubled by the mechanics of songwriting.)

Two contrasting views of musical education are presented in the documentary. Chambers studied classical piano and composition at the Guildhall School of Music and Drama in London, and attributes his facility with the mechanics of songwriting to the education he received. "Don't bore us, get to the chorus", he tells Wainwright. Wainwright's lack of formal training is also revealed, as he gleefully seizes upon this line, and insists on incorporating it into the chorus of 'World War III'. Chambers shows concern at the exposure of an "insider trick" for writing successful songs, of which Wainwright seems blissfully unaware. Yet, on testing 'World War III' with BBC radio commissioners and hosts, the consensus is that the words scan and that the line could be taken as referring to an insider club of which membership is desirable.

Among the influential songwriters interviewed for the documentary is Diane Warren, who has achieved mainstream success with her single-authored and co-written songs in a variety of genres.[5] Over her career, Warren acquired extensive musical and harmonic knowledge, but she learnt the trade by ear rather than by attending music college. Some of her comments throughout the BBC documentary betray anxieties about the lack of legitimization from the popular music world: Warren's concern with "doing stuff that's wrong", or "not the correct way", betrays an inbuilt belief that a formal education is the only way to success in music (*Secrets of the Pop Song*, 48:09). And yet her awards for songwriting speak for themselves – and she is also aware of the importance of retaining her personal style and "go[ing] where my heart tells me to go". Her contradictory belief that receiving formal songwriting/compositional training would erode this ability is apparent.

'Pretty Things'

Wainwright's promotion of the song 'Pretty Things', from *Want One*, as a twenty-first-century Lied makes a further association with the "father of the Lied":

> The song is really important because I want to keep the modern
> lieder [sic][6] aspect of solo voice and piano alive. I want it to be one
> of the foundations of my career. I'm very influenced by Schubert.
> Someone said there's more beauty and expression in two bars of a
> Schubert lieder [*sic*] than in a four-hour opera. (Wainwright, 2003)

'Pretty Things' exhibits a more explicit Schubertian compositional influence than 'Imaginary Love'. The song is in simple verse form. It is orchestrated for acoustic piano and voice, with piano chords marking out a crotchet pulse throughout. The song is in 4/4 throughout, excepting short meter changes to 3/4 (heard in verse 1 at 0:35, and verse 2 at 1:12) and 2/4 (in verse 3, at 2:17). Despite these time changes and Wainwright's rubato performance style, the crotchet pulse is clearly articulated. Table 2.2 shows the song structure.

Table 2.2: 'Pretty Things', song structure

Piano introduction
Vocal pick-up (0:04)
Verse 1 (0:08)
Verse 2 (0:46)
Piano interlude (1:28)
Verse 3 (1:34)
Coda (2:21, ends at 2:41)

Again, Wainwright uses rubato and phrase extension to disguise a simple song form: the sixteen-bar verse 1 begins after the song's piano introduction (0:08), consisting of two repetitions of an A phrase with a small vocal range, a B phrase with more extensive vocal range and metrical shift, and a repeat of the A phrase. Verse 2 (0:46) is a straightforward repetition of this musical material, and is followed by a short piano interlude (resolving the song back to the opening key of F major). Verse 3 is constructed from similar musical material to verses 1 and 2, but is structured, with a structural alteration making it ABBA. Verse 3 is followed by a short coda (phrase A) to finish. The song remains close to the home key of F, with subdominant suspensions contributing to a hymnal quality. A trope of mainstream popular music is present in the four-chord loop at the opening. The first two verses feature limited harmonic and melodic motion, with inversions of Bbmaj^7 (subdominant major 7) and D minor (relative minor), shown in Figure 2.3. More expansive harmonic vocabulary is contained in verse 3 (1:34), in which Wainwright utilizes Eb^7/Db, Cm and Gm as modulatory pivot chords, before resolving with a perfect cadence of Cm–C–F.

The lines "Pretty things, so what if I like pretty things/Pretty lies, so what if I like pretty lies" (verse 1) give an insight into Wainwright's character. He continues by lamenting his alienation from society and from his loved one: "From where you are/To where I am now". It is but a small step to unite the two lyrical features: a man who is attracted to the typically feminine "pretty things" is bound to be ostracized and alienated from society. Kevin C. Schwandt draws a connection between the isolating and ostracizing device of Wainwright's protagonist's taste for pretty things (going against the masculine norm), and a musicological

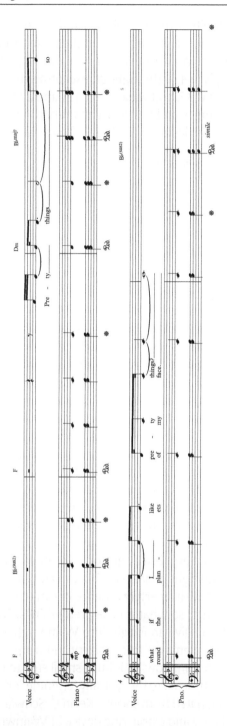

Figure 2.3: 'Pretty Things' extract

reading of Schubert as Beethoven's feminine Other. Schwandt suggests that by associating himself and his music with Schubert, Wainwright implicitly aligns himself with these domestic and feminine readings (2010: 170).[7]

Schwandt goes on to argue that Wainwright was no doubt aware of the academic controversy concerning the homosexual dimension of Schubert's life and music (2010: 159–70). 'Pretty Things' connects Wainwright's contemporary songwriting with the historical tradition of alienation and oppression associated with homosexuality. In his later output Rufus Wainwright also explains his dissatisfaction with contemporary American intolerance in the song 'Going to a Town' (discussed in Chapter 3).

Wainwright is taciturn about his creative process. However, close analysis of these two songs, cross-referenced with information gleaned from documentaries and interviews, shows that his song forms and harmonic changes are straightforward, while his lyrics are complex and multi-referential. This suggests that he creates the textual content before the musical content, providing similarities with composers such as Schubert, who set pre-existing poetry to music for his song cycles.

Yellow Lounge

In 2007, Wainwright made a further connection between his own music and career and that of Schubert. He was invited to take part in the record label Deutsche Grammophon's Yellow Lounge series: an occasional Berlin club night devoted to classical music, for which prominent popular musicians are asked to compile a playlist. Martin Hossbach, the former product manager for the Classical Department of Universal Music, explains:

> In a nut-shell, this was the concept: to present classical music not in a concert hall but instead in special locations not normally associated with such music. [Concept developer] De Sera wanted to use the Yellow Lounge to attract a new, younger audience to the world of classical music by employing contemporary, modern methods of presentation. (Hossbach, 2007: 10)

Wainwright's playlist contained a predictable selection of operatic passages from Verdi, Puccini and Wagner, as well as more eclectic classical music from Haydn and Rameau, and esoteric choices including Ravel's Concerto for Left Hand Piano (see Table 2.3 for track listing). Wainwright's playlist was bookended by his own piano quintet arrangements of his pop songs, performed by the Fauré Quartet with piano. His inclusion of his own pop music alongside such eminent classical composers shows that he is placing himself alongside the western art music tradition. By removing his most identifiable popular music characteristic, his voice (discussed in more detail in Chapter 5), and by providing some of the superficial trappings of art music, he enabled his music to be heard in the same way. The quintet arrangements are arranged and performed in line with western classical performance values, with vibrato, warmth of sound, precise intonation and clear moments of ensemble blend and soloistic clarity. Yet, paradoxically, by juxtaposing arrangements of his popular songs with repertoire from the established classical canon, a paucity of musical content is revealed. Wainwright's popular songs do not contain the same musical development of ideas as repertoire by Tschaikowsky, Beethoven *et al*. The musical content of Wainwright's popular song is simpler than western classical music. His performance style is bombastic and nuanced, which adds colour and emotion to the musical materials. In contract, classical performers are trained to be clean and precise in their performance style – nuance is created in repertoire from the western art music canon by the depth and complexity of musical materials (effectively, in pop, the "song" materials can be simple, because the "performance" will bring it to life. In classical music, the "performance" is often clean and precise, but the detail in the "song" or score will energize it.) The classical performance of Wainwright's pop songs on his Yellow Lounge choice does not achieve the musical intensity of standard pop *or* classical performances. A blend between the classical and popular music art worlds could more realistically be achieved by beginning from the ground up, and applying knowledge and skills from both repertoires.

More familiarity with the western art music world is apparent in Wainwright's choice of pre-existing repertoire. His inclusion of 'Auf dem Flusse', a central Lied in Schubert's cycle *Winterreise*, is particularly interesting. The lyrics and music of 'Auf dem Flusse' portray a flowing brook as an ominous threat, while the *Winterreise* cycle as a whole features the "winter's journey" of a socially isolated man. As Youens commented, Schubert's choice of poetic subject was often autobiographical in nature (1997: 103). Wainwright's focus on Schubert can be seen to mirror and augment Schubert's autobiographical themes, as well as his own. His frequent references to Schubert in 'Imaginary Love', 'Pretty Things' and the Yellow Lounge show an engagement with the same themes of love, loss, isolation from society and oppression.

In the mid-2000s, Rufus Wainwright began to make a parallel name for himself in the art music world. In 2005 New York choreographer and dancer Stephen Petronio set contemporary dance to 'Oh What a World'. *Bud* was performed at the Joyce Theatre in New York on 22 March 2005. The following year, Petronio and Wainwright expanded this setting to four songs, to feature a small cast of dancers performing to 'Oh What a World', 'Vibrate', 'This Love Affair' and 'Agnus Dei'. Rather than depicting a clear narrative, the work as a whole was intended to be representative of a series of mental states.

Table 2.3: Rufus Wainwright Yellow Lounge track listing[8]

1. Wainwright, *Hometown Waltz*
2. Tschaikowsky, [*sic*] *Eugen Onegin: Polonaise*
3. Beethoven, *Symphonie Nr. 6: Szene am Bach*
4. Berlioz, *Les Nuits d'ét*
5. Schubert, *Winterreise: Auf dem Flusse*
6. Verdi, *Messa da Requiem: Rex tremendae*
7. Haydn, *Streichquartett, op. 20 Nr 1: 3. Satz*
8. J. S. Bach, *Brandenburgisches Konzert Nr. 1: 3. Satz*
9. Rameau, *Les Indes galantes: Danse des Sauvages*
10. Puccini, *Tosca: Tre sbirri, una carroza*
11. Elgar, *Enigma-Variationen: Andante*
12. Elgar, *Enigma-Variationen: I. (C. A. E..): L'istesso tempo*
13. Elgar, *Enigma-Variationen: VII. (Troyte): Presto*
14. Ravel, *Klavierkonzert für die linke Hand: Finale*
15. Wagner, *Götterdämmerung: Siegfried's Rheinfahrt*
16. Schnittke, *Quasi una sonata*
17. R. Strauss, *Salome: Ah! Ich habe deinen Mund geküsst*
18. Schostakowitch, [*sic*] *Symphonie Nr. 5: 3. Satz*
19. Wainwright, *Cigarettes and Chocolate Milk*

In her review of the *Bud Suite* for the *New York Times* (2006), Jennifer Dunning commented on the "elusive undercurrent of sexuality" that pervaded the piece, which opened with a sensual male duet set to 'Oh What a World' (carried over from *Bud*). Lisa Haight's review of *Bud Suite/Bloom* performed in London's Queen Elizabeth Hall in October 2006 made explicit the "mixture of frenzied movements that successfully fused contemporary [dance] and ballet" (2006). The shedding of an established art world (ballet) for new developments (contemporary dance) was echoed in the dancers' discarding of traditional costume for modern garb, as Haight describes:

> Four women with their backs to the audience wearing red lycra shorts with red and pink tutus on their rears and white shirts with a[n] "x" on the back moved together and connected with each other ... Two women then left the stage and tore off the remaining women's tutus. (2006)

Haight's review is overwhelmingly positive ("one of the most mesmerising [pieces] I've ever seen"), and she explains how Rufus Wainwright's music complemented the stylistic blend of choreography. By collaborating with artistic figures who shared his multiplicity of artistic influences, Wainwright began to bring together classical and contemporary art worlds.

This performance also featured a further collaboration. Petronio commissioned a new score from Wainwright for *BLOOM*, which featured musical settings of a Latin mass as well as poetry by Walt Whitman and Emily Dickinson. Performed by Petronio's dance company and the Young People's Chorus of New York City, *BLOOM* explored the tribulations and liberations experienced in the transition from childhood to adulthood. *BLOOM* also premiered at the Joyce Theatre in New York on 18 April 2006.[9]

Petronio categorizes his pieces as contemporary dance, not ballet. He vehemently opposes classical training, stating:

> The story of my life is, I had no training, and that has been my gift ... That I (a) didn't let it get in my way, (b) was arrogant enough not to care, or stupid enough not to care, and (c) had some good advice. I had people around me saying you don't have to become a bad ballet dancer to become successful. (La Rocca, 2006)

A parallel can be seen between Petronio's views on the conflict between retaining his artistic identity over training in an established idiom, and Rufus Wainwright's rejection of attending music college or studying music at university.

Sonnette

Wainwright's next art music project was a collaboration with the American experimental theatre designer, playwright and opera director Robert Wilson. Wilson's most famous artistic endeavour is his 1976 collaboration with New York minimalist composer Philip Glass on *Einstein on the Beach*, an opera in four acts, connected by five "knee plays", or intermezzos. Like Petronio's *Bud*, *Bud Suite* and *BLOOM*, *Einstein on the Beach* is formalist in structure, containing a series of events rather than a continuous narrative. Wainwright's collaboration with Wilson – known as *Sonnette* – was a setting of twenty-four Shakespeare sonnets to music accompanying avant-garde theatre and dance, performed by the Berliner ensemble in Berlin in April 2009.[10] The production was extremely stylized, with fourteen members of the Berliner Ensemble elaborately costumed and made up as characters from Shakespeare's plays. Again, there was not a clear narrative trajectory. The production was focused instead on striking appearances, featuring exaggerated costumes and hairstyles, thick black and white makeup, and making use of character silhouettes. Many characters' gender identity was blurred: Christine Dreschsler and Anna Graenzer played young boys, for example, and Dejan Bucin played a character credited as "Gentleman/Lady".

Rufus Wainwright draws upon many influences in his musical settings of Wilson's chosen sonnets: as well as his soundscape of acoustic piano and solo voice, the accompanying sound worlds range from medieval plucked lute, folksong-like acoustic guitar, rock-based electric guitar and drums, to Weillian stomping basslines and vocal recitative. The vocal delivery ranges from spoken narrative and *Sprechstimme* to musical-theatre style delivery and rawly emotional rock.[11] Some sonnets are translated into German, some are introduced in German recitative, and some remain in English. In an interview with the Berlin magazine *Tip*, Wainwright credited his artistic influences:

> The idea of this commissioned piece of the [Berliner Ensemble] came from the dramaturg Jutta Ferbes. But I knew Bob Wilson for years too and always wanted to work with him. On top of that I am a big Kurt Weill and Brecht fan: that's why the combination of Bob Wilson, Shakespeare and working with the theatre was very tempting. (Behrend, 2009)

Wainwright's use of the German language is suitable for the Berliner Ensemble and their audience in Berlin, and creates a link to Weill's musical theatre. However, avid discussion on Rufus Wainwright's fan message boards debated the merits of changing the language in which Shakespeare is heard. A brief cross-section of message-board comments in the months leading up to the Berlin première of *Sonnette* illustrates the diversity and intensity of fan opinion:

> Hyperufusensitive: "Will it all be in German? I have nothing against German, really its [*sic*] just I'm rather used to reading (and hearing) Shakespear[e] in English."
> Kathquadmum: "I had a feeling that the sonnets would be translated into German ... as a native English speaker ... and [S]hak[e]speare fan ... this distresses me intensely ... I am saddened that Robert [W]ilson and [R]ufus agreed to do this ... I can't bear Wagner in English so why the hell translate Shakespeare into German [?] Shakespeare is such an important writer ... it doesn't mean the same in another language and Rufus wrote the music to the [E]nglish ... and it will lose something in translation."
> Isabella1: "Shakespeare in German. Bad news."
> PocketPenniless: "A travesty ... There are such strict constraints to a sonnet."
> Toddland: "We know Rufus doesn't [speak German]. It just seems very strange to me that Rufus would agree to do this if they were gonna translate it. [H]e wouldn't translate Prima Donna precisely because he said the music and words were so entwined."

> polleke: "I'm sorry, but for me this language thing is a non issue. Both Rufus and Robert Wilson are equal to quality. So no matter what, I still look forward to this event, no matter if it is in Englisch [*sic*] or German."
> Nutmeg3000: "I think this will be the same for most of the audience ... They are theatre people and possibly don't worry too much about the music."
> (http://forums.rufuswainwright.com/index.php?/topic/41412-shakespeare-sonnets-berlin-april-2009/page__st__280, 11–12 March 2009, last accessed 17 February 2014)

Wainwright's oeuvre encourages his listeners to challenge traditional binaries between western art music and commercial popular song. By integrating the two art forms in a number of ways – from art-music inflected pop songs, to the use of these songs in a ballet, to *Sonnette* – his work encourages audiences, fans and scholars to think outside expected generic boundaries.

Prima Donna

Prima Donna marked Rufus Wainwright's first single-authored foray into the classical music world. Peter Gelb, who took on the role of general manager of the New York Metropolitan Opera in 2006, had a forward thinking and progressive outlook. He had previously – and controversially – promoted classical "crossover" recordings as head of Sony Classical. Soon after accepting the position with the New York Metropolitan Opera, he commissioned contemporary operatic projects from numerous key modern figures, including American jazz trumpeter Wynton Marsalis, British film composer Rachel Portman and the Argentine classical composer Osvaldo Golijov. In 2007, he suggested to Rufus Wainwright that he write a contemporary American opera. Wainwright enthusiastically leapt at the chance to embrace one of his passions. Wainwright chose to write the libretto in French, assisted by French author, translator and singer-songwriter Bernadette Colomine. The use of the French language reaffirmed his Canadian family roots, as well as aligning him with the tradition of his operatic idols. For example, on top of developing and reinforcing the nineteenth-century Italian operatic style, Verdi wrote six French-language operas (such as *Les vêpres Siciliennes*). While Wainwright's French language choice aligned him with the art music world, it ultimately made the project unsuitable for the Metropolitan Opera, whose management hoped for a contemporary *American* (i.e. English language) work that would appeal to younger audiences. As a result, by late 2007 Alex Poots (director of the Manchester International Festival [MIF] in Britain) and Wainwright entered discussions about using the Opera North Orchestra to perform the première of *Prima Donna*.

By this time, Scottish soprano Janis Kelly had heard about the project, and already privately expressed her support for it to Rufus Wainwright.[12] She had sung with Opera North for many years, and at the time was singing with the Grange Park summer opera programme in Hampshire, in southern England. In an interview in summer 2013, she recalled that Poots and an organizing team from the MIF travelled to Northington to hear her sing the Foreign Princess in Dvorak's *Rusalka*, and arranged for her to meet with Wainwright. Kelly secured the principal role after a short audition and discussion.

Prima Donna portrays an opera singer's decline. The central character, Régine St. Laurent, is returning to the operatic stage to reprise the role that made her career, after a six-year retirement. The plot focuses on her preparations and anxieties before the performance, and her interactions with a small handful of other characters: her maid Marie (played in the première by soprano Rebecca Bottone), her butler Philippe (baritone Jonathan Summers) and the journalist André (tenor William Joyner). Régine eventually loses her nerve, and her voice, before the reprise of the role. Many reviewers drew parallels with Maria Callas's vocal decline in her later years (this connection is explored further in Chapter 3).

Conductor Pierre-André Valade explained some of the difficulties faced by Wainwright in composing and mounting this large-scale pursuit:

> It comes from someone who knows opera from the outside, and who has never written for an orchestra, and I must say it's quite challenging for someone who's writing their first piece for an orchestra to write an opera. It's quite a mad idea. It's incredible … The most difficult [thing we're facing] is actually the musical aspect, and getting through to Rufus, and getting to understand each other. (Scott, 2009: 45:36–53:48)

I asked Kelly about the extent of Wainwright's authorial voice in the creative process. She explained that Bryan Senti, a composer and conductor of Columbian parentage who studied music at Carnegie Mellon and Yale University, had been brought in to help Wainwright with musical processes and orchestration for *Prima Donna*. Senti was still a graduate student at the time. Kelly stated:

> Bryan Senti sat with Rufus and more or less wrote down, or put on paper, what Rufus wanted. It wasn't a case of handing over to an orchestrator. Which, I have to say, some composers still do … He had to learn about orchestration, and had to learn about instruments. And he would say to himself, it might not be the perfect orchestration of what he wanted, but he had a full seventy-piece orchestra at his disposal, and he wanted to make absolute use of them

> the whole time … We had balance problems at times, and he didn't
> want it miked. So over the years, little bits here and there have been
> tweaked, in order to make it easier. (Kelly, 2013)

This quotation from Kelly alludes to help received by Wainwright from the experienced musicians and directors involved. In her note of support, she had offered to help with the tessitura (expected range) of a soprano voice, something that is doubly important here because it is an opera about an opera singer. A typical dramatic soprano range is B_3 to C_6 – the role of Régine at times demands low Gs, and the 'Vocalize' of Act II demands a portamento (smooth transition between two recognized pitches) with a range of a ninth. This suggests that Rufus Wainwright had an imperfect command of the technical demands of a dramatic soprano, as illustrated by some of Kelly's comments:

> I know for sure that he'd already asked Renée Fleming to do it. She
> would never sing that low in public. It has got lots of low bits in it,
> for a soprano … There were a couple of places where she [Regine]
> was doing her exercises in front. We compromised on those. There
> were a few scales really high, almost too close together to be able to
> take a decent breath. (*Ibid.*)

There is a fine line between challenging musical content and unidiomatic/ unsingable writing. Having offered her help in defining the soprano's range, Kelly insists that *Prima Donna* is vocally challenging in a constructive way, rather than being unsingable, stating: "It tests you vocally in all sorts of ways, so it's a really good thing to keep your voice exercised with … She [Régine] is very much on my piano stand" (*ibid.*).

Amongst Wainwright's collaborators and close circle, *Prima Donna* was deemed a success. His decision to compose an opera received his mother's steadfast support. Kate comments: "I think a lot of people would think it would be a folk opera, but it really does fall into the category of grand opera, just because that's what he's used to listening to" (Scott, 2009: 1:47). This comment shares the common understanding that grand opera is any operatic production that employs larger forces than a chamber opera. In fact, grand opera has its own set of traditions and techniques, many of which Wainwright does not employ in *Prima Donna*. David Charlton explains the many uses of the term "grand opera" by different musicians and critics in different countries over the nineteenth century. In *The Cambridge Companion to Grand Opera*, he reflects these historical differences of opinion, and recognizes common elements: "historical crisis, a personal tragedy, regional character (focused through local musical colour), active choruses, dance and political imperatives refracted from the distant past towards the composers present" (2003: xiii). Wainwright's production does not include a chorus, ballets, or a clearly outlined political context, so cannot be placed into the category of grand opera. I asked Janis Kelly if *Prima Donna* belongs in the operatic canon, and she vehemently replied in the affirmative, stating: "it is as difficult at times as Strauss, Massenet, Poulenc ... I still hope that [Placido] Domingo will want to do it in L.A." (Kelly, 2013).

Prima Donna premiered on 10 July 2009, at the Manchester International Festival, performed by the Opera North chorus and orchestra. It has two acts, with an overture to each one (see Table 2.4). Act I closes with an instrumental interlude, behind which the romantic backstory plays out. Act II begins with an overture, and contains two instrumental interludes (at II-6 and II-11). The placement of these interludes is suggestive of the Verdian incorporation of ballets or the early nineteenth-century operatic tradition of including intermezzi in grand opera, aligning Wainwright further with the music of his idol. The opera contains twelve arias, of which six belong to Régine, including the closing aria 'Les feux d'artifice', which recalls the fireworks in Paris on Bastille Day. A solo aria, rather than a large ensemble piece, to close is one way in which Wainwright's opera differs from nineteenth-century Italian grand opera, but as will be shown later, this song was beneficial to his career. Twelve of Wainwright's thirty-seven musical numbers are scored for two voices. *Prima Donna* also contains four trios, and two full ensemble quartets. One of these quartets, Act I, Scene 21 'Oh, ma douleur' provides the dramatic ensemble finale that was a regular feature of Verdian opera.

Although Rufus Wainwright was eventually listed as the sole composer and author of *Prima Donna*, the production team contained at least four collaborators: along with Colomine, there were orchestration assistant Bryan Senti, conductor Pierre-André Valade and director Daniel Kramer. Wainwright's lack of formal musical education worked against him in this large-scale project. George Scott's 2009 documentary about the making of *Prima Donna* shows Wainwright bewildered and exasperated by traditional musical terms and techniques, as the orchestrator helps him to realize his vision.

Having numerous collaborators does not invalidate the piece or Wainwright's claim of authorship. Indeed, I would argue that the extended creative team further places Rufus Wainwright in the classical music world. Collaboration is a long-established tradition in opera – Verdi, for example, had a raft of collaborators and assistants. The text of his *Macbeth* (Florence 1847) came to Verdi through a prose translation by Carlo Rusconi, and featured a libretto by Francesco Maria Piave and revisions by Andrea Maffei, and the opera was later revised in French for a performance at the Paris Opera in 1865. A non-Verdian example of a collaborative opera is Giacomo Puccini's *Manon Lescaut* (1893), which featured two librettists (Luigi Illica and Domenico Oliva) after Antoine-Françoise Prévost's novel.

Table 2.4: *Prima Donna*: Acts, scenes and musical numbers

Overture to Act I: Instrumental

Act I, Scene 1: 'Oh! Madame Saint Laurent' (Marie, Madame; duet)

Act I, Scene 2: 'J'ai rêvé toute a nuit' (Madame; aria)

Act I, Scene 3: 'Merci' (Marie, Madame; duet)

Act I, Scene 4: 'Ah! Les soucis' (Marie, Madame; duet)

Act I, Scene 5: 'Aliénor' (Madame; aria)

Act I, Scene 6: 'Mais non, Madame!' (Marie, Madame; duet)

Act I, Scene 7: 'Mais que se pass-t-il donc ici?' (Marie, Madame, Philippe; trio)

Act I, Scene 8: 'A lépoque, François avant' (Philippe; aria)

Act I, Scene 9: 'Cet appartement' (Philippe; aria)

Act I, Scene 10: 'Mon dieu qu'il est laid!' (Philippe; aria)

Act I, Scene 11: 'À ton âge, François' (Philippe; aria)

Act I, Scene 12: 'Voici le journaliste' (Andre, Philippe; duet)

Act I, Scene 13: 'Bonjour, Madame Saint Laurent' (Madame, Andre; duet)

Act I, Scene 14: 'Quant j'étais jeune étudiant' (Madame, Andre; duet)

Act I, Scene 15: 'Madame Saint Laurent de-puis combine de temps' (Madame, Andre; duet)

Act I, Scene 16: 'La prémiere' (Marie, Madame, Andre, Philippe; quartet/ensemble)

Act I, Scene 17: 'Régine' (Madame, Andre; duet)

Act I, Scene 18: 'Abandonne, pose ta couronne' (Andre; aria)

Act I, Scene 19: 'Charmont, tout à fait' (Madame, Andre; duet)

Act I, Scene 20: 'Oh, ma voix!' (Marie, Philippe; duet)

Act I, Scene 21: 'Oh, ma douleur' (Marie, Madame, Andre, Philippe; quartet/ensemble)

Act I, Scene 22: Interlude

Act I, Scene 23: The Kiss (no singing)

Overture to Act II: Instrumental

Act II, Scene 1: 'Dans ma pays de Picardie' (Marie; aria)

Act II, Scene 2: 'Excusez-moi!' (Marie, Philippe; duet)

Act II, Scene 3: 'Vocalize' (Madame; aria)

Act II, Scene 4: 'Quand j'étais jeune étudiant' (Madame; aria)

Act II, Scene 5: 'Dans ce jardin' (Madame, Andre; duet)

Act II, Scene 6: Interlude (instrumental)

Act II, Scene 7: 'C'est impossible' (Marie, Madame, Philippe; trio)

Act II, Scene 8: 'Maintenant il est temp' (Madame, Andre, Philippe; trio)

Act II, Scene 9: 'Je suis heureuse' (Maria, Madame, Andre; trio)

Act II, Scene 10: 'Prenez-le donc' (Madame; aria)

Act II, Scene 11: Final interlude (instrumental)

Act II, Scene 12: 'Les feux d'artifice' (Madame; aria)

Collaborative help for *Prima Donna* also came from director Daniel Kramer, who added significant dramatic sections, including a romantic backstory. Kramer said:

> The biggest challenge is the libretto and the story, and getting him [RW] to be passionate about dramatic action and relationships, and growth, and the theatre of opera. He's very interested in the music of opera but I think less in the theatre of opera, and we've been pushing for that all along. (Scott, 2009: 56:40)

Kramer's perception that Wainwright was more interested in the sounds and themes of opera than in the musical and dramatic substance is telling. Wainwright was able to create a convincing reproduction of the musical worlds he claims to have been surrounded by as a child, but did not have the rigorous training and knowledge required to create all the details of an opera. After its première, *Prima Donna* was extensively revised after damning reviews from the classical musical establishment. The revised version has a small performance history that includes showings at Sadler's Wells (UK, April 2010), Luminato Festival Toronto (Canada, June 2010) and Brooklyn Academy of Music (New York, February 2012), and concert performances of extracts within Wainwright's own live shows.

Most professional classical music critics considered the piece seriously lacking in musical and emotional content. In April 2010, Andrew Clements (music critic for the British broadsheet newspaper *The Guardian*) explained his own thoughts on Wainwright being turned down for writing in French, and his opinion of the shortcomings of the revised version of *Prima Donna*:

> The Metropolitan Opera in New York reportedly turned down Wainwright's opera because he insisted on setting the libretto ... in French. Yet the more one hears of the score, the more one could imagine that as a tactful exit strategy, preferable to rejecting the work because of its shortcomings. *Prima Donna* is the work of a man who loves opera and the sensations it delivers, without understanding how it is paced, or how it generates dramatic tension. (2010)

Clements ends his review by deeming *Prima Donna* "the worst new opera I've ever seen" (*ibid.*). Clements's underlying implication is that being an opera fan does not entitle one to join the canon. The opinion of the cognoscenti is that Wainwright alludes stylistically to a number of opera composers, but does not bolster this with the knowledge of the idiom that could be gained from years of rigorous study of the tradition.

All Days are Nights

Wainwright's next album, released in March 2010, reflected his turbulent personal life. *All Days are Nights: Songs for Lulu* was a melancholic, pensive song cycle for solo voice and piano, placing him immediately in a lineage including Schubert's *Winterreise* and Robert Schumann's *Dichterliebe*. However, the album was released as an album using popular music marketing strategies, making it an example of art music and popular music aesthetics converging. The album's title further reinforces Wainwright's art music concerns: "All days are nights" is a line from Shakespeare's Sonnet 43, Wainwright's setting of which forms track 6 of the album. It is one of three Shakespeare settings on the album that were first made for *Sonnette*. 'Songs for Lulu' references the eponymous female protagonist of Alban Berg's 1936 twelve-tone opera, who is at times a snake, a maneater, a prostitute, and murderer – her protean personality echoing the "poses" of Wainwright's second album.

The overall mood of the album is dark, with the front page of the CD booklet featuring a single eye, heavily lined in kohl, and looking into the middle distance. This is almost mirrored on the back page; here the eye is even more heavily made up, featuring spiky eyelashes and is half-closed and bloodshot. The central page reveals this to be part of a full portrait of Wainwright, in which one half of his face is made up and in shade, while the other half is unadorned and in natural light. This duality mirrors the idea of multiple personalities alluded to by the poses on the 2001 album, and by Lulu. Wainwright's facial expression is mournful, perhaps reflecting the events of his personal life. The split portrait is a reflection of the musical content of the album: Rufus Wainwright is visually identifiable from his portrait because half of his face is bare, while musical characteristics such as the timbre of his voice and his habit of referring to his family in song ensure that he is recognizable even in this stripped-back and simple presentation.

The text of the CD booklet is in a stylized and artistic handwriting, underscoring the emotional investment in the album. The personal resonance of the album is highlighted further by the handwriting credit to Jörn Weisbrodt. The inside title page contains white handwriting on a black background. This is inverted on the inner pages, containing the lyrics and dedication: "To Martha, the Bright Lady", he writes. An analysis of the lengthier dedication to Kate can be found in Chapter 5.

The tour that accompanied *All Days are Nights* featured an art music-like performance, with Wainwright sitting onstage in a darkened auditorium, dressed in a dark theatrical costume, playing and singing acoustically at the piano. In performance, he would request that audiences refrain from applauding until the end of the cycle, ensuring that the artistic continuity was unbroken.

Rufus Wainwright's art music concerns are furthered in the recording and engineering of the album: it was engineered by Tom Schick for Decca, and produced by Wainwright.[13] Universal Music Group (the company that bought DreamWorks in 2005) bought Decca in 1998.[14] Decca is renowned for its classical recordings, having released the stereo recordings of Ernest Ansermet conducting L'Orchestra de la Suisse Romande, and employing producer John Culshaw from 1946. Culshaw revolutionized the world of opera recording, promoting a much more naturalistic recording technique than the common practice of simply placing a microphone in the room with a singer. By releasing *All Days are Nights* with Decca, Wainwright places himself further into the art music world.

All Days are Nights contains twelve songs (see Table 2.5) for solo piano and voice. This aligns Wainwright with the Lied of Schubert and Schumann, and continues the lineage of singer-songwriters accompanying themselves in the popular music world. More specifically, by continuing the tradition of singer-songwriters accompanying themselves, and by aligning himself with the art music ideal of the song cycle, Wainwright created a direct musical connection to his early collaborator, Van Dyke Parks. Parks's early success can be attributed to the album entitled *Song Cycle* (1968), which featured a mélange of styles including folk, baroque, experimental rock and pop, and psychedelia. Wainwright's DreamWorks Records co-founder Lenny Waronker produced *Song Cycle*. Parks's album is an early example of art music aesthetics meeting popular music marketing: by taking the idiom's name as the title of his album, Parks indicated an art music ideology and large-scale production values that Wainwright would perpetuate.

Table 2.5: All Days are Nights: Songs for Lulu track listing

I:	Who Are You New York?
II:	Sad With What I Have
III:	Martha
IV:	Give Me What I Want and Give It To Me Now!
V:	True Loves
VI:	Sonnet 43: When Most I Wink
VII:	Sonnet 20: A Woman's Fire
VIII:	Sonnet 10: For Shame
IX:	The Dream
X:	What Would I Ever Do With a Rose?
XI:	Les Feux d'Artifice t'Appellent
XII:	Zebulon

American singer-songwriter Tori Amos had similar art music aspirations with her 2011 release *Night of Hunters*.[15] Like Wainwright, Amos has a personal history with classical music: she gained a scholarship to study classical piano at the preparatory department of Baltimore's Peabody Conservatory. And while Wainwright dropped out of McGill University's Music Department to pursue songwriting and performance ambitions, Amos lost her scholarship at the age of eleven, something she attributes to her burgeoning appetite for rock and popular music.[16] Like Wainwright and Diane Warren, in some ways Amos prided herself on not having a grasp of the intellectualized aspects of musical education; the fact that her 1980s synthpop band and their 1987 eponymous album were both called *Y Kan't Tori Read* emphasized this. Amos regularly accompanies herself on piano, and her albums feature virtuosic and idiosyncratic piano parts, which suggest musical training although, like Wainwright, she did not remain in formal education for long. Angela Watercutter describes *Night of Hunters* as a "21st century interpretation of a traditional song cycle based entirely on classical themes" (Watercutter, 2011). Like *All Days are Nights*, a record label famous for its classical repertoire released the album: in this case, Deutsche Grammophon, "the world's most celebrated classical music label" (Amos, 2011). The classical music sound world is furthered by Amos's exclusive use of acoustic orchestral instruments.

Amos utilizes the song cycle format in a more orthodox way than Wainwright, creating an over-arching narrative throughout the fourteen songs of the album. In her case, the protagonist is a woman

> who finds herself in the dying embers of a relationship. In the course of one night she goes through an initiation of sorts that leads her to reinvent herself, allowing the listener to follow her on a journey to explore complex musical and emotional subject matter. (Amos, 2011)

Amos's daughter and niece play secondary characters in the narrative. A similarity to Wainwright's use of members of his close and extended family can be seen: the difference is in Amos's creation of distinct characters in the song cycle for her family members, whereas Wainwright's family perform backing vocals.

In their contemporary (and contemporaneous) albums, Wainwright and Amos adopt the nineteenth-century idiom of the song cycle in different ways. Both artists accompany themselves on piano, but Wainwright's sole use of piano to back his vocals is more attuned to the nineteenth-century Lieder of Schubert and Schumann than Amos's classical chamber orchestra. The large-scale programmatic narrative of *Night of Hunters* is in line idiomatically with cycles such as *Winterreise* and *Die schöne Müllerin*, portraying an arc of emotion similar to the nineteenth-century stories of love and loss. *All Days are Nights*, on the other hand, is fragmented in its use of subject matter, ranging from autobiographical songs to songs created for other purposes. Yet one could argue that Amos's use of several pre-existing musical themes is as fragmented as Wainwright's choice of topics.[17]

Wainwright's piano and voice sound world provides coherence, yet in other areas, *All Days are Nights* is less cohesive. The album has no large-scale tonal progression. Nos. 6, 7 and 8 were written and previously performed as part of 2009's *Sonnette*. No. 11, 'Les feux d'artifice t'appellent', could previously be heard as Madame's Act II, Scene 1 aria in *Prima Donna*. Lyrically, the cycle is fragmented, with some new songs referring to specific autobiographical instances, and others to large-scale philosophical questions.

All Days are Nights/Songs for Lulu is the only complete Rufus Wainwright album to be published as sheet music. The art music ideology of the song cycle, and of the Decca recording, is reflected in the manner in which it is published. The cycle is presented in a matte yellow book, with a plain cover simply announcing the title, the composer's name and the publisher in black font. The inner pages are matte ivory, and in keeping with score traditions from classical music, give the composer's full name and birth year. After a written introduction by Wainwright, the songs are listed on a contents page. The lyrics are then printed, and finally the piano and vocal scores, which contain a mix of Italian and English musical terms. In the introduction to the score, Wainwright explains the trials and tribulations of his personal life at the time of writing:

> This song cycle represents the vortex of what so far has been the darkest and brightest time of my life. The impending and eventual death of my mother, the great Kate McGarrigle, from a rare form of cancer called clear cell sarcoma, occurred simultaneously with the production of my first opera *Prima Donna*, my fulfilling work with Robert Wilson and the Berliner Ensemble on the Sonnets project, and eventually – last but certainly not least – the joyous birth of my daughter Viva Katherine. All of these milestones imbue this music's emotional core with life's anchor of experience, and behind every song there is a story that singers and pianists alike will glimpse if they choose to look. But now that I've lived through these events and the songs are finally free for others to perform with this publication, I hope that artists choose to divorce themselves completely from my personal story and embrace the sounds and melodies of *Songs for Lulu* to fit their own experience, since in the end, we all live fabulously emotional and complex lives. That is my wish. (Wainwright, 2012)

Conclusion

This chapter has suggested that there are two musical worlds present in Rufus Wainwright's output and career. Western art music references and devices pervade his popular output, as demonstrated by the analysis of 'Imaginary Love' and 'Pretty Things'. Despite their art music influences, however, these songs adhere strictly to popular song forms as defined by Covach and Flory – 'Imaginary Love' is in contrasting verse-chorus form, and 'Pretty Things' in simple verse form.

All Days are Nights sold fewer copies than Wainwright's previous albums because, to some degree, it alienated both Wainwright's popular music fans and the art music audience. The album was marketed as a contemporary popular music album, yet its aesthetic belongs to late nineteenth-/early twentieth-century classical music. But while popular music audiences are happy to hear references to art music, they respond badly to art music disguised as pop. His art music enterprises were initially influenced by his commercial activities, but the two became increasingly divorced as his career progressed. Perhaps it is enough for him to be separately successful in each category, or in Janis Kelly's words, "to wear two hats" (2013).

3 Opera, Gender and Sexuality

> Since I was 14 years old I have been converted to the dark religion of opera. I'll even be dramatic about it: it has saved my life, guiding me through some pretty tough junctures.
>
> (Wainwright in Higgins, 2008)

Rufus Wainwright associates his awareness of his homosexuality with discovering opera in his teens: the connection between gay men and opera was also made explicit by influential literary figures in the early 1990s. Important texts in this tradition include Wayne Koestenbaum's *The Queen's Throat: Opera, Homosexuality and the Mystery of Desire* (1993), and Sam Abel's response *Opera in the Flesh: Sexuality in Operatic Performance* (1996).

Wainwright's teenage obsession with the idiom manifested itself in several ways: he listened compulsively to Verdi in his bedroom; re-enacted *Tosca* with his sister and cousins; and recalled playing a recording of *Norma* loudly through the car stereo on a family holiday to Martha's Vineyard in Massachusetts, the hometown of Jacqueline Kennedy, widow of the former US president.[1]

Operatic references and techniques in his music became more frequent once Wainwright's musical career began to gain momentum, and these references are almost always connected with expressions of his sexuality. The following discussion of five of his commercially released popular songs (the recorded tracks are discussed here, unless otherwise explained) and music videos suggest how he uses operatic tropes to play with expected constructions of sexuality. Juxtaposing the operatic tropes in Wainwright's commercial output and music videos with scholarly readings from traditional musicology (particularly the "new musicology" of the 1990s and beyond) can offer insights into both fields.

Operatic Protagonists: 'Damned Ladies', 'April Fools'

'Damned Ladies', included on Wainwright's demo tape and later released on his debut album, features eight operatic protagonists as they head towards their fictional deaths. Sophie Muller, who directed the music video for 'April Fools' (released as a single from the same album), saw the cinematic potential of this narrative and re-located it to modern-day Los Angeles. The surfeit of *femmes fatales* invites a consideration of Catherine Clément's *Opera, or the Undoing of Women*, where the opera stage is portrayed as a site in which "women perpetually sing their eternal undoing" (1988: 5), and Carolyn Abbate's riposte "Opera: Or, the Envoicing of Women" (1995).

Wainwright directs the lyrics of 'Damned Ladies' to the operatic heroines, alluding to the method of their deaths, and mourning the inevitability of their fate. The repeated refrain "Why don't you ladies believe me when I'm screaming/I always believe you" indicates his level of emotional investment in these figures, and his frustration at the inevitability of their deaths. Here is he echoing a sentiment first expressed by Clément, who suggests that male librettists, composers, directors and producers have created an art form in which audiences are invited to witness "the great masculine scheme surrounding this spectacle thought up to adore, but also kill, the feminine character" (1988: 6). Her standpoint goes some way to explaining why women (and feminists of either gender) could feel empathy and sadness for operatic heroines.[2]

In *The Queen's Throat* the American poet and cultural critic Wayne Koestenbaum offered an explanation of the oft-cited and under-theorized affinity homosexual men have with opera. Reclaiming the slang term "opera queen" for homosexual men who love opera, Koestenbaum suggests several manifestations of the phenomenon. He proposes that the opera queen enjoys the ritualistic glamour and pageantry of grand opera (which is referenced by the House of Rufus tagline "velvet, glamour and g[u]ilt"); he suggests conversely that opera recordings provide relief from the implicit oppression of a heterosexual society; that opera divas provide a focal point for obsession; and above all, that the music of opera prompts a physiological response in homosexual men (Koestenbaum, 1993).

Clément's and Koestenbaum's scholarship go some way towards explaining why Wainwright uses such frequent operatic references in his songs. In 'Damned Ladies', his engagement with the deaths (rather than the music) of operatic protagonists can be aligned with that of Clément, who unashamedly states:

> I am going to talk about women and their operatic stories. I am going to commit the sacrilege of listening to the words, reading the libretti, following the twisted tangled plots ... *initially* this is not to be about the music. (1988: 12)

"Desdemona, do not go to sleep" he sings, evoking the central female character in Verdi's *Otello* (1887). He implies that if she did not slumber, she could not be awoken and inevitably strangled by Othello. The plot Verdi uses for *Otello* is adapted slightly from William Shakespeare's *Othello*: Shakespeare's Desdemona is smothered to death, while Verdi's Desdemona's violent strangling is dramatically better suited to the operatic stage.

"Brown-eyed Tosca, don't believe the creep" refers to the tricks and mind games exerted upon Puccini's Tosca (1900) by Baron Scarpia, resulting in the execution of her lover Cavaradossi and her subsequent suicide (she jumps off a castle parapet). "Violetta, keep your man locked up", he sings to the principal figure in Verdi's *La Traviata* (1852), "Or like Cio-Cio you will end up burned by love or sickness", he explains, alluding to Violetta's eventual death from consumption. Cio-Cio San is the Japanese female protagonist in Puccini's *Madama Butterfly* (1904), who commits a ritualistic Japanese suicide – cutting her throat with her father's *hara-kiri* knife – after being entrapped and deceived by an American husband. "There is a knock at the door/Tell me it's not Mimi again" refers to a central female character in Puccini's *La Bohème* (1896), who escapes from the bohemian underworld of Paris to live with a wealthy lover, before dying of tuberculosis. "Or is it Gilda's waiting passion to be stabbed and killed again?" sings Wainwright. Gilda is the beautiful daughter of the title character of Verdi's *Rigoletto* (1851), who, after a complicated network of love and deception, is stabbed by an assassin hired by her father to kill her lover. "Kát'a Kabanová, why did you marry him?" relates to the eponymous heroine of Leos Janáček's 1921 opera, who drowns herself after realizing that she is in love with someone other than her husband. The final figure in Wainwright's roll call of heroines is Pamina, from Mozart's *The Magic Flute* (1791). Pamina's is the only positive story in this catalogue of disasters – Wainwright sings "Pamina got away from mama", recalling the plot device by which Pamina evades the plans of her mother (the Queen of the Night) to sacrifice her to the evil Monostatos.

Operatic protagonists also feature in the only music video released with the debut album *Rufus Wainwright*. As mentioned above, Sophie Muller was hired to direct a video for the third song on the album, 'April Fools'. The song features a rhythmic backdrop of synthesizer, piano and guitar. The lyrics are a tongue-in-cheek commentary on the nature of love, with the catchy hook "You will believe in love". The juxtaposition of multiple operatic plots made the narrative of 'Damned Ladies' a suitably cinematically complex choice for the music video. The video begins with Rufus waking up in a double bed in a house in modern-day Los Angeles, surrounded by five opera heroines. As he wakes, Rufus stretches his left arm, which has been draped across his chest. A gold wedding ring is clearly visible, distancing him from the homosexuality implied by Koestenbaum's opera queens. The year after Koestenbaum's book was published, Paul Robinson commented on the frequency with which opera can be associated with ambiguous sexuality, suggesting that this is a factor in opera queens' affinity with the idiom:

> What started by looking like a clear-cut matter of sexual attraction turns into something more resembling identification – moreover, identification, be it noted, with a singer of ambiguous gender. Indeed, one begins to suspect that precisely the ambiguities of gender, or what is now called gender construction, lie at the heart of the association of opera with homosexuality. (1994: 287)

The opera heroines in the 'April Fools' video can be identified by their attire and makeup, as well as through the nature of their demise. Violetta, pale and dressed in black, sneezes into a handkerchief. Rufus walks to a grand piano to sing the refrain "You will believe in love". Initially, the girls stay close to him, maintaining as much contact as possible, and singing backing vocals. The group walks down the street, and Rufus supports Violetta as she doubles over coughing. She is the first to die, and he embraces her, before leaving her in the street and proceeding with the remaining heroines. The group enters a diner and Rufus looks at the menu while Gilda fans herself. Gilda looks Italianate, with striking features and dark hair. A man (we presume her lover, or her assassin) rushes in, gives her flowers, and tries to pull her away from the table. Rufus tries to stop him, but the man pulls her upright and stabs her. A knife falls to the floor. Meanwhile, Tosca runs out of the diner and throws herself from an overpass. Rufus rushes after her, but reaches her too late, and looks mournfully at her prostrate body. He cannot keep up with the number of operatic protagonists hurtling towards their inevitable deaths. Cio-Cio San (played by Martha, dressed in a kimono and white makeup, with chopsticks in her hair) lays out a bamboo mat in the aisle of the diner. She gets out paraphernalia for her ritualistic suicide, unsheathes a dagger, and kills herself. Rufus arrives, anguished, moments after her death. The scene cuts to Mimi, who is being harassed by a group of motorcyclists. She dies on the street, covered by her black cloak. When Rufus finds her he appears distraught. Images are shown of all the bodies scattered around Los Angeles. Rufus prods Cio-Cio San, who revives and jumps up, holding his hand and running after him. All the protagonists come back to life and can be seen sitting around a table with Rufus, drinking wine and laughing. He crawls back into the double bed and they join him, returning to the exact frame that opened the video. The circularity of the plot suggests that the fantastical plot could be a dream – calling into question the wedding ring that he wears on his left hand. The resurrection of the leading ladies also reflects the way in which female opera singers mime their own deaths on stage every night, before coming back to life for the curtain call and the following night's performance.

Opera is aligned with sexuality here, for not only is Rufus celebrating the female protagonists of numerous opera plots, but his obsession also reinforces facets of Koestenbaum's opera queen. Wainwright's evident frustration at his inability to save the figures from their scripted deaths is echoed in Clément's observation that opera is a one-way art form. Audiences are compelled to listen and watch the planned action – they do not have the power to change the outcome (1988: 6–7).

'Barcelona'

Later in her text, Clément explains the connection between opera heroines and outsiders:

> Their original desire, their sadness, their violence, their necessary lies are not communicable in the country where they are living. From this inner exile is born the sweet lament that enhances Carmen's charm when she sings and dances, Violetta's cries when she decides to die of love, Mélisande's silence, and Butterfly's suicidal purity. The return to their country can only be accomplished in death, suffering, or betrayal. (1988: 67)

Social ostracization and isolation are features of several operatic plots (for example, Puccini's *Madame Butterfly*, Verdi's *Don Carlos* and Britten's *Peter Grimes*). Wainwright's adoption of such plot devices in his popular songs shows an awareness of the dramatic techniques of opera.

'Barcelona', featured on 1998's *Rufus Wainwright*, is deceptively simple both musically and lyrically. At 6:54, the song is more than twice as long as standard three-minute pop songs (a format established in the early twentieth century, when songs were created to fit on one side of a 78rpm record). Indeed, 'Barcelona' has a compound ABA song structure, with one complete simple verse song form inside another (the song structure is laid out in Table 3.1). Verses A1 and A2 (0:00–1:14) are resolved by verse A3 at the end of the song (5:58–6:54). The song opens with an acoustic guitar figure, cello countermelody and wordless backing vocals. Wainwright paints a picture of an unfriendly city and deserted apartment, before closing each verse with the refrain "Fuggi regal fantasima" ("flee, regal ghost"). The Italian lyric is a quotation from Verdi's *Macbeth*, and comes from the moment when Macbeth believes he has seen the ghost of Banquo. As David Metzer observes, musical quotation evokes cultural associations – both with the newly created work, and those attributed to the quoted work (2003: 7).[3]

Wainwright has spoken in interviews about the parallel he sees between the vital operatic ingredients of love, drama and death. He came out and grew up in the midst of the 1980s paranoia and hysteria about AIDS (acquired immune deficiency syndrome), which was often directed towards homosexual activity. The operatic themes of love, drama and death can also be found in the social (mis)awareness of AIDS, and as such, 'Barcelona' can be understood on one level as a description of a gloomy sojourn in a deserted city, and on another level as an extended metaphor for the disease. Wainwright has explained that the 1990s was a frightening time to be growing up in the homosexual community. The royal ghost he refers to can be read as the spectre of AIDS hanging over his lifestyle: Lake makes this connection explicit, suggesting that "Rufus tak[ing] Macbeth's cry ... at the site of Banquo's unborn sons [is] a device to articulate his sheer terror of AIDS" (2009: 109).

Table 3.1: 'Barcelona', song structure

Instrumental introduction:	0:00
Verse A1:	0:11
Refrain A:	0:31
Verse A2:	0:42
Refrain A:	1:03
Rubato introductory couplet:	1:15
Verse B1:	2:01
Refrain B:	3:05
Verse B2:	3:41
Refrain B:	4:44
Rubato closing couplet:	5:32
Verse A3:	5:58
Refrain A:	6:26 (ends 6:54)

Lyrics such as "all the crows got panderers" and "Don't want my rings to fall off my fingers" explicitly connect sex with death, and they associate a flamboyant lifestyle in which Wainwright wears rings with a disease in which the jewellery may not stay on his wasted fingers. A Verdian parallel can again be drawn with the consumption afflicting *La Traviata*'s Violetta.

An introductory and closing couplet frames verses B1 and B2, which feature contrasting melodies, rubato and many internal lyrical repeats. In particular, Wainwright repeats the phrase "But I fear it's a long way down" as a refrain to both verses. More musical layers are added, as piano, flute, castanets and overdubbed vocal lines join. Again, Wainwright's lyrics simultaneously describe the city of Barcelona and the unpredictability of AIDS. "Even if that straw I pull/[means] I got to fight a bull", he sings – evoking stereotypical images of Spain but also alluding to the chance of a deadly encounter. The line "in Spain Don Juan's to blame" places the responsibility for the assumed predicament on a libertine – situating the song both in Barcelona and within operatic history (for Don Juan is the subject of a number of operas).

The final verse (5:58–6:54) is a repeat of the opening verse and accompaniment, closing the opening song. The lyrics – referring to organizing his papers, laying out summer clothes and closing his suitcase – can be read as a metaphor for getting his affairs in order before a trip, or before death. The idea of closing his suitcase echoes the metaphor of baggage expounded in 'Want' (discussed in Chapter 1), showing that he can leave this place or this world with a light conscience. On the final iteration of "Fuggi regal fantasima", all parts (melody, and instrumental and vocal accompaniments) slow and fade dynamically to end with silence.

'Going to a Town'

Wainwright moved to Berlin to begin to record his 2007 album *Release the Stars*. He had initially planned a streamlined pop venture, after the extravagance of the *Want* albums. However, as Lake writes:

> The new minimalist Rufus' head had been turned by the romantic possibilities of the German and Austrian countryside ... Germany was the land of the great Wagnerian composers and he was always more in thrall to soaring Wagnerian towers than he was to Bowie and Eno's concrete bunkers and broken glass ... he ended up in made-to-measure lederhosen arranging string quartets and vocal harmonies. (2009: 235–36)

Release the Stars featured several of the city's freelance classical musicians, who valued the expressivity and liberation to be found in the recording techniques and musical styles of an artist rooted in the pop world.

In the second song on the album, 'Going to a Town', Wainwright makes the themes of isolation, alienation and oppression more explicit. The song contains a slow-moving backdrop of repeated piano chords, bass and drums. Backing figures on electric guitar, and *arco* (bowed) and *pizzicato* (plucked) strings get more complex and involved as the song progresses. Lyrically, it is a direct criticism of the Bush government, and the pro-war, anti-homosexual attitudes propagated by its supporters. Lines such as "I'm going to a town that has already been burnt down/I'm going to a place that has already been disgraced" spell out the fact that he considers America to have deteriorated beyond reprieve, and prepares listeners for the refrain "I'm so tired of you America".

'Going to a Town' was released as a single with an accompanying music video in early 2007. Sophie Muller again directed the music video, which is heavily symbolic: Rufus languishes in a prison cell (symbolizing oppression), which is furnished with only a simple table and chair, and a golden vase of red roses (representing martyrdom). As the song progresses, pictures of falling rose petals are projected against the wall, resembling spilled blood. Extramusical factors contribute to a nuanced reading of the video – in particular, the props and setting. Three ghostly female backing singers, dressed in black, join him. Oppression is again apparent, as Rufus answers their request "Tell me" with the explicit "do you really think you go to hell for having loved?" The three women are veiled, but occasional close-up shots reveal facial expressions of anguish. Close-up shots also reveal racial differences – the central woman is black, and her grimace is more severe than that of the other two, again suggesting oppression. While Rufus Wainwright's homosexuality could be hidden, sedate clothes cannot hide her difference from the white American norm. The women's appearance is effective but ambiguous: they could represent the three witches of Macbeth (linking the song back to the Verdian quotation in 'Barcelona'), or they could represent some of the operatic heroines in Muller's 1998 video for 'April Fools'. Wainwright is clearly mourning his society (as are the three women), while pointing out the sometimes shortsighted and overzealous religious fervour and political prejudice towards the homosexual community in America. At the end of the song, the three women place a laurel crown upon his head (denoting Jesus), and pull him into a standing crucifixion position, implying that he must be martyred for his country and values.

Despite the repeated line "I'm so tired of you, America", 'Going to a Town' is not geographically specific. The lyrical and visual content (of the song and music video respectively) suggest several interpretations. The first interpretation (and the interpretation to which my reading so far is most closely aligned) is of a criticism of the Bush government in general. The "town" is never named, and the song can be taken to be a general dissatisfaction with American society and culture. The second possible interpretation (and one favoured by many members of Rufus Wainwright's officially sanctioned fan forum) is that the song concerns New Orleans, specifically in the aftermath of 2005's Hurricane Katrina. Hurricane Katrina caused extensive damage and destruction to New Orleans in August 2005, not least by disrupting the underground network of gas pipes. The resulting gas leaks inevitably caught fire, resulting in "a town that has already been burnt down". Arguably, President Bush's failure to respond quickly to the disaster with financial aid meant that the town was also figuratively burnt down – abandoned by the central government. Yet another interpretation of 'Going to a Town' is the idea that it refers to Berlin. Not only was the album recorded in Berlin, but also the burning of the Reichstag on 27 February 1933 is irrevocably associated with the beginning of Hitler's dictatorship. The Nazis capitalized on the culture of fear engendered by the Reichstag Fire, claiming it was the beginning of a Communist revolution, and Hitler, who had been sworn in as Chancellor four weeks earlier, used the event as the reason to suspend civil liberties and trigger mass arrests of Communists. The arson attack and the consequent suspension of democratic representation of the people (Communist members of the Reichstag were arrested, giving the Nazis a majority in the newly homeless Parliament) represents the "town that has already been burnt down", while themes of persecution and oppression easily can be transposed from the subsequent anti-Semitism in 1930s Germany to homophobia in 2000s America. With 'Going to a Town', Wainwright implicitly makes a connection between the past and the present, and between different geographical regions of destruction and oppression.

'Greek Song'

The desire to be elsewhere is expressed with varying degrees of explicitness in 'Barcelona', 'Damned Ladies'/'April Fools' and 'Going to a Town'. Wainwright makes this clear through his lyrical and musical allusions to Europe – which he consistently associated with opera.

These allusions position him as an outsider within the American rock mainstream – highlighting his difference. Difference, too, is an operatic trope. Since the art form's beginnings, dramatic conflict has been created by juxtaposing a central, mainstream community of characters against a minority outsider. Difference is manifested to varying extents in the outsider, who is either female or geographically removed (or, increasingly, both). In 1991, Ralph P. Locke defined this trope as the "Oriental 'Other'", using the case study of Saint-Saëns's *Samson et Dalila*. He suggested that musical devices connoting Orientalism reference both the female and geographic "Other". The operatic device of musical exoticism to denote the outsider is used in Rufus Wainwright's rock output to denote the gendered outsider. His position against the masculine heteronormative standard can be conflated with his European ideology.

'Greek Song' is the second song on Wainwright's 2001 album *Poses*. However, even in his explicit attempt to write in a more conventional style, Wainwright brought in elements of the operatic that play with his construction of sexuality; in this case, Orientalism and the outsider.

The narrative structure of the song is that of a love duet between Wainwright (if the song is – as usual – assumed to be autobiographical) and a Greek man. The song documents a holiday affair, and explains a decision the pair needed to make at the end of their time together. Table 3.2 explains the song structure, where each verse consists of the same musical material, and the chorus contrasts.

Table 3.2: 'Greek Song', song structure

Instrumental Introduction:	0:00
Verse 1:	0:23
Verse 2:	0:35
Verse 3:	0:47
Verse 4:	0:59
Chorus:	1:11
Instrumental:	1:36
Verse 5:	1:48
Verse 6:	2:00
Verse 7:	2:12
Verse 8:	2:24
Chorus:	2:36
Chorus:	2:48
Instrumental to fade:	3, ends 3:59

The lyrics take the form of a duet, as the subject position of each consecutive verse alternates between Rufus and that of his lover (see Table 3.3). However, Wainwright sings the entirety – describing a situation in which he has the upper hand. This vocal device also has the effect of constructing an operatic "Other" – Wainwright sings his own verses from the standpoint of the Western norm, while portraying his lover as an exotic Other. However, his singing style and inflection stay the same, meaning that the listener has to pay attention to catch the intricacies, and implying that there is less separation between him and his lover than is implied by the music.

Table 3.3: 'Greek Song', verses 1–2

You who were born with the sun above your shoulders
You turn me on, you turn me on you have to know
You who were born where the sun she keeps her distance
You turn me on, you turn me on but so does she
You who were born there where beauty is existence
You turn me on, you turn me on your body heals my soul
You who were born where you shiver and you shudder
You turn me on the girl is gone so come on, let's go

There are many things of interest in this short extract. The repetitive nature of the lyrics, whereby changing the last few words of a repeated phrase creates a different meaning, is similar to blues improvisation. In her book *Saying Something: Jazz Improvisation and Interaction*, Ingrid Monson emphasizes the conversational properties of improvisation, in which musicians within an ensemble might repeat each other's musical ideas, modifying the ends of phrases to give their own personal touch:

> The function of repetition in creating a participatory musical frame-
> work against which highly idiosyncratic and innovative improvisa-
> tion can take place has often been lost upon otherwise sympathetic
> commentators ... This relationship between formal linguistic devices
> and their practical use in social interactions offers us an important
> point of comparison to the relationship between formal musi-
> cal structures and their emotional, aesthetic, and cultural feeling.
> (1996: 89–90)

The "Otherness" of Wainwright's voiceless lover is reinforced through the non-verbal music. An exotic sound world is established in the instrumental introduction to the first verse. As Matthew J. Jones writes:

> The song begins with guitars and dobro playing [a] repeated rhyth-
> mic cell over a simple harmony while the percussion contribute[s]
> something like a South American clave rhythm gone awry. When
> the piano introduces a pentatonic flourish, which becomes the basis
> for a violin counterpart later in the song, Wainwright seems to have
> collapsed a number of Others into an amalgam of difference with
> no regard to actual Greek music. Though Wainwright's ensem-
> ble uses some Western counterparts for traditional Greek instru-
> ments ... the confusion of pentatonic scales, clave-like percussion,
> and other Western instruments can be interpreted as an Orientalist
> attitude, wherein regional, ethnic, and cultural differences are inter-
> changeable. (2002: 104–105)

The use of generic non-Western musical features to represent any geo-graphical "Other" is a technique lifted wholesale from nineteenth-century French opera. Ralph Locke's commentary upon *Samson et Dalila* is entirely applicable to 'Greek Song'. In the case of both Wainwright and Saint-Saëns, it is possible to see examples of "general stylistic aberrations ... applied indis-criminately by composers to vastly different geographical settings" (Locke, 1991: 261). McClary concurs, considering the phenomenon from a French perspective. She remarks that Spain, North Africa and the Orient were largely interchangeable, and explains that by the mid nineteenth-century a "code" had developed for depicting the Orient in music (1992: 51–53). According to German musicologist Carl Dahlhaus,

> regardless of the milieu being depicted, exoticism ... almost invari-
> ably [made] do with the same technical devices: pentatonicism, the
> Dorian sixth and Mixolydian seventh, the raised second and aug-
> mented fourth, nonfunctional chromatic coloration, and finally bass
> drones, ostinatos, and pedal points as central axes. (1989: 306)

Much has been made in the popular press of Wainwright's openness about his homosexuality and lifestyle, and about the fact that he sings from a gay perspective in his music. Given that fact, the explicit suggestion of a homosexual relationship in 'Greek Song' is unsurprising.

More surprising is the presence of a third person in this holiday relationship. The final line of the second stanza, in Wainwright's voice, is "you turn me on, you turn me on, but so does she". Earlier in the verse, he allocates the sun a feminine pronoun ("the sun she keeps her distance"), suggesting that the first verse alludes to sun worshipping. The second verse (Wainwright singing in the Greek's voice) explicitly states that "the girl is gone" in the following stanza. The ambiguity of "she" in the first verse becomes a specific woman in the second. The implication is that the Greek is already in a heterosexual relationship, and that the holiday relationship alluded to represents not just a break from the norm for Wainwright's persona but for that of the Greek. The remainder of the song offers two sets of possibilities, as the man must decide whether to pursue a life with Wainwright or remain with his family and partner.

The poignancy of Wainwright wishing to stay with the Greek, who wishes to leave Greece to travel with Wainwright, is acute – there seems to be no possible positive outcome of the situation. References to "either side" suggest the decision the boy has to make about the future of his sexuality. The boy fears violence, suggesting homophobia in his home country: he is certain that someone is waiting "prepared to strike", and he is "scared to death". In the end, though, Wainwright advises him to "save your poison for a lover who is on your side". Which "side" that may be is left ambiguous. Wainwright uses the operatic devices of Orientalism and the construction of an exotic Other in his rock song to portray fluid and multifarious versions of masculinity. The ambiguity of the lyrical content forces the listener to consider the questions raised.

'Vibrate'

The opening of *Want One*'s 'Vibrate' features a habanera bassline, played acoustically by *pizzicato* double bass and doubled by piano. The habanera form began as a stately English country dance in the 1700s, before being exported to continental Europe and to Haiti via France (Barulich and Fairley, n.d.). The habanera uses a duple metre, a dotted, arpeggiated bass line, and two repeated eight-bar sections. The most famous use of the form in western art music was by the French composer Georges Bizet in his 1875 opera *Carmen*.[4]

The eponymous female protagonist is one of opera's most famous femme fatales, controversial at the time because of her louche morals and laissez-faire attitude to love. As Peter Robinson comments: "The most obvious threat [to the established male-dominated society] is Carmen's sexuality" (1992: 10). She has remained a striking figure of liberation in cultural consciousness. This loucheness is epitomized in her first musical appearance in the opera, her aria to Don Juan 'L'amour est un oiseau rebelle', for which Bizet drew upon a Cuban version of the dance (again, showing the interchangeability of exotic cultures at the time). Figure 3.1 shows the typical habanera bass line, as used in 'L'amour est un oiseau rebelle'. Figure 3.2 shows the similarities to the acoustic bass line to Wainwright's 'Vibrate'. His use of the habanera conjures up associations with Carmen. Through his use of this musical form, Wainwright suggests an ambiguous sexuality: his voice is male, but the operatic device implies the sexuality, love and death usually associated with female operatic protagonists.

Figure 3.1: Habanera bass line

Figure 3.2: 'Vibrate' bass line, transcription KW

'Vibrate' is faithful to the habanera form, and more specifically to Bizet's 'L'amour est une oiseau rebelle'. However, subtle musical and lyrical differences illustrate Wainwright's juxtaposition of aspects of popular music and western art music. 'Vibrate' is in 3/4, in contrast to Bizet's traditional 2/4. In popular music terminology, Wainwright's song is in simple verse form, where each verse consists of two eight-bar phrases that are consistent with the habancra form (the song structure is shown in Table 3.4). Verses 1–3 use the same harmonic and melodic material, while verse 4 consists of a contrasting vocal melody over the same harmonies. Verse 4 is differentiated still by a caesura (pause) on the word "anytime" (2:01–2:03), and a contrasting, yearning emphasis on the leading note of the scale (2:11–2:25). Bizet, on the other hand, adheres to the traditional habanera alternation of musical material for each subsequent verse, featuring different orchestral textures and call and response phrases as the aria proceeds. Like Bizet, Wainwright begins each verse with a pickup, beginning the melody three quavers before the beginning of the bar. Each vocal section is separated by four bars (two repeats) of the modified habanera bass – truncated at either end by an overspill of the vocal melody. In combination with the metrical shift created by his rubato and the pauses in verse 4 (discussed later), this is rhythmically unsettling. Wainwright adds a new instrumental or vocal texture to support the melody in each verse: woodwind in verse 2, strings in verse 3 and wordless vocals in verse 4.

Table 3.4: 'Vibrate', song structure

Instrumental Introduction:	0:00
Verse 1:	0:05
Verse 2:	0:36
Verse 3:	1:07
Verse 4:	1:39
Partial Reprise:	2:09 (ends at 2:41)

The lyrics themselves provide few clues about the subject's masculinity or otherwise. The message of the song is clear: the protagonist, hoping for a phone call from a lover or loved one, keeps their mobile phone on vibrate in anticipation. The vibrate function is a personal alert – drawing attention by bodily sensation rather than aural interruption, highlighted by lyrics such as "still I never ever feel from you".

Rufus Wainwright frequently slurs his words, blurring vowels into indiscriminate sounds. As Jones writes: "He sings with an affected diction, quite distinct from that of his speaking voice with long, nasal vowels, and soft consonants that often completely disappear, muddying his lyrics considerably" (2002: 81). As such, a word in the penultimate line of the first verse is swallowed: "I'd like to dance ... Britney Spears", he sings. "I guess I'm getting on in years". This elusive word adds more ambiguity to the construction: "I'd like to dance *to* Britney Spears" implies a protagonist of either gender. "I'd like to dance *with* Britney Spears": again, either this statement could come from either gender. "I'd like to dance *like* Britney Spears" would probably be sung by a female, or by a man in touch with his feminine side. Bearing in mind that 'Vibrate' is played out entirely over the aforementioned habanera bass line, Wainwright again uses operatic devices to suggest sexual ambiguity.

A Barthesian reading of Wainwright's unusual singing diction is informative here. In his 1977 article "The Grain of the Voice", Roland Barthes draws a distinction between two types of singer and recorded song. He builds on Julia Kristeva's definitions of "geno-text" and "pheno-text", suggesting that "geno-song" is the expression of emotions through the articulation of the language used. The physical production of the words and music (which Barthes sees as one) imbues the delivery with expressive meaning. On the other hand "pheno-song" refers to "features which belong to the structure of the language being sung" (1977: 182): the rules of the genre, the performer's adherence to expectations of the form, the composer's particular style. Barthes suggests that pheno-song expresses conventional emotions through the coded forms of its delivery. Rufus Wainwright's slurred vocal style can be categorized as geno-song: the delivery confirms that it is music of the body and not of the soul. Wainwright's diction and singing style inspire jouissance rather than conventional pleasure.

The Queen's Throat is relevant here: Koestenbaum begins with a catalogue of defining characteristics of an "opera queen"; indeed, one of the characteristics he proposes is that "the opera queens keep lists" (1993: 17). For the purposes of the current discussion of opera and sexuality, I focus on his idea that "the opera queen must choose one diva":

> The other divas may be admired, enjoyed, even loved. But only one diva can reign in the opera queen's heart; only one diva can have the power to describe a listener's life, as a compass describes a circle. (*Ibid.*: 19)

Koestenbaum's chosen diva is clear: Chapter 4 is titled "The Callas Cult", and devoted entirely to his infatuation with Maria Callas. He explains Callas's importance to gay culture, and to him personally:

> She was Callas long before she died, but she would be a little less Callas if she were still living. Untimely death assists her legend and connects her to themes that have shadowed gay culture: premature mortality, evanescence, solitude ... Callas became an international star in the early 1950s, a time when gay people, though silent and secret, and seeking assimilation and acceptance rather than radical action, were developing a rich culture. Callas remains the operatic diva most closely (if only tacitly) associated with gay fandom. (Many Callas commentators are gay; virtually none consider gayness worth mentioning.) (*Ibid.*: 134–35)

Wainwright's own association with Callas is complex and multi-faceted. The version of the song released on *Want One* features a long, high, sustained note on the last iteration of the word "vibrate" (Figure 3.3). It is possible to hear his voice straining at the end of the held note, and he has been known to crack the note or run out of air in live performance. Wainwright has referred to this as his "Maria Callas moment" (Lake, 2009: 183), for its operatic overtones. (As a side note, this musical effect once again associates Wainwright's habanera with Bizet's – Carmen's melody line features a high-pitched sustained note towards the end of verses 1 and 2, creating musical and emotional drama.)

Figure 3.3: Final iteration of 'Vibrate', transcription KW

It is clear that Wainwright admires Callas, but the relationship is not straightforward. By juxtaposing 'Vibrate' with Koestenbaum's "Callas Cult", it is possible to nuance this relationship. Koestenbaum writes: "I worship her because she made mistakes, and because she seemed to value expressivity over loveliness" (1993: 136). Grover-Friedlander concurs: "The public's adoration exceeds the quality of her singing" (2006: 45). In his own "Maria Callas moment", Wainwright acknowledges the importance of the opera diva and prima donna to gay men. By composing and recording his own version, though, rather than worshipping and commenting from afar (*pace* Koestenbaum), he writes himself into the history of prima donnas. An affinity with, rather than a strict adherence to, the opera queen is apparent.

Prima Donna
Rufus Wainwright's obsession with the traditions, creators and figureheads of opera is epitomized by *Prima Donna*. In July 2009, Wainwright arrived at the première of his opera at the Palace Theatre in Manchester, UK, dressed as Giuseppe Verdi "complete with frock coat and beard" (Sturges, 2012: 13).

Inspiration for the plot came from a BBC documentary from 1968. *The Callas Conversations* gave Wainwright the idea of centring it around a prima donna, considering the first woman's personality as well as her vocal prowess. The narrative opens with the fictional prima donna in question recalling her former glory, before a comeback performance after six years of retirement. The female protagonist was modelled on his family members and Maria Callas: "Janis is the lead character. In many ways, that character is a composite of myself, of my mother, of my sister in a way" (Scott, 2009: 3:45). In 2013, Janis Kelly asserted that: "There's bits of Callas, definitely bits of Callas in there."

Smith suggests that writing *Prima Donna* cemented Wainwright into the history of opera queendom: "Wainwright is himself a self-identified opera queen, and one who has attained what might be considered the holy grail of operatic-queendom, having actually written his first opera" (2013).[5]

I disagree. Wainwright's affinity with opera is not a closeted adoration as described by Koestenbaum, Morris and Smith. By writing his own opera, Wainwright composed himself into the operatic tradition. He had long been preparing for this moment via the narrative focus of 'Damned Ladies' (and the video to 'April Fools'), and the operatic themes of oppression and loneliness in 'Barcelona' and 'Going to a Town'. Geographical displacement is revisited in 'Greek Song', with misery and a lack of resolution for both Wainwright and his voiceless Greek lover. Many commentators associate voicelessness with Maria Callas, for she famously lost her voice in her later years.

This chapter both began and ends with Callas's impact on Wainwright. His self-announced "Maria Callas moment" comes at the end of 'Vibrate', a song subtly connected to opera on many musical levels. Again, though, Wainwright is not obsessing over a diva from a distance. He is using the musical techniques associated with her to write himself into the history of opera.

4   Place and Space

Evocations of place and space play an important role in Rufus Wainwright's music. I use the terms "place" and "space" carefully, to differentiate between characterizations of identified locations, including specific buildings as tourist or nostalgic sites ("place"), and to depict non-specific landscapes, cityscapes and buildings, including those that connote performance venues ("space"). Several of the songs discussed contain explicit references to geographical spaces, both in and outside America: 'Barcelona' (see Chapter 3) conjures the desolate streets of the eponymous city, while 'Montauk' (see Chapter 5) evokes the domesticity of family life in Long Island. Other songs, such as 'Greek Song', evoke exoticism and ethnic sounds, without verbally describing the place. The distance from a loved one, and the desire to be in a different location, are referenced in the lyrics to 'Vibrate' and 'Going to a Town' respectively (all discussed in Chapter 3).

In recent years, musicologists have increasingly explored the relationship between music, place and space.[1] By engaging with this literature, and expounding my own theories about the significance of geography in popular music, this chapter investigates the impulses conveyed by Wainwright's music and actions. To my mind, place and space influence popular music in four main ways, and in this chapter I deal with each of these consecutively. Firstly, the notion of a music scene as defined by Sara Cohen (1999) applies to Rufus Wainwright's early performance days on the club circuits of Montreal and New York City. Secondly, I consider the development and perpetuation of regional styles in popular music.

Thirdly, I evaluate Wainwright's musical representations of place and space. In song, there are two possible ways of musically representing geographical attributes: either by describing the place in question in lyrical content – usually used to characterize the former; or by musically depicting the topography of a space – which illustrates the latter. Krims regards the former as a blunt tool of evocation: which "involves [music's] lyrical and musical characterization of cities, i.e. involves representation" (2007: xxxiv). Finally, I consider the venues within which Rufus Wainwright performs, and how these may carry cultural connotations that affect the music produced and audience response.

Music Scenes

An important variation on the idea of place in popular music is the concept of a musical *scene*. Sara Cohen defines a musical scene thus:

> The scene is not just a social and material entity. It is also a meaningful concept defined and interpreted in a variety of ways. Some suggest that rock culture in Liverpool can be labelled a 'scene' only if 'something is happening' – if local bands are being signed up by record companies and there is coverage of the local scene in the national music press, if good local performance venues exist that can stimulate music activity and act as the scene's 'heart' or 'core', if the production of local rock music can be characterized as communal and collaborative rather than fragmented and fractional, or if there exists an identifiable and distinctive local musical sound or style. The notion of a local rock scene can thus be related to a romantic ideology familiar to rock culture, and link[ed] with issues of authenticity, difference, and community. (1999: 241–42)

Wainwright began his performance career by playing in small local Montreal clubs. Yet the idiosyncrasy of his musical content and performance style did not adhere to an existing "scene" as defined by Cohen. His style drew from many geographical regions, and a brief explanation of the different cities in which his seven studio albums were recorded shows the geographical diversity, or rootlessness, of his recording career.

Wainwright's musical style was influenced by several idioms (including 1960s folk, opera and cabaret), resulting in an anachronism and an eclecticism that did not invite comparisons with contemporaneous musicians, and meant that his music did not fall into an easily recognizable scene. Lake writes:

> With bands like the Red Hot Chili Peppers, REM and the Smashing Pumpkins all over alternative and college rock, Rufus would have to compete for gigs and record deals with those bands' ever-hopeful, undiscovered, generally never-to-be-discovered soundalikes. He certainly didn't fit in with the alternative rock scene, and contrary to the expectations of those aware of Rufus' family history, his music did not sit any more comfortably with those on the traditional folk circuit. (2009: 70)

Wainwright's songs frequently refer to his family members and lovers, but he rarely makes direct reference to famous contemporary figures or events, placing them into a vacuum of time. This characteristic is usual in mainstream popular song, as Davis writes in her guide to lyric writing: "A standard is a song that maintains its popularity years after its initial success because the lyric's sentiment exerts a timeless appeal" (1985: 5). Exceptions to this in Wainwright's popular song include his tribute to the deceased River Phoenix ('Matinee Idol', *Rufus Wainwright*), 'Natasha', addressed to the actress Natasha Lyonne, verbal references to actors Jane Curtin and John Lithgow in 'Want' (both from *Want One*), and songs dedicated to his publicist Barbara Charone and the actress Rashida Jones ('Barbara' and 'Rashida' from *Out of the Game*).

After beginning his performing career in small Montreal clubs, as noted earlier he went to stay with Loudon in New York City in 1993. There he spent time at venues such as the Crow Bar in the East Village. Singer-songwriter Jeff Buckley had been based in New York since February 1990, exploring similar venues. Wainwright frequently found his own budding career as a singer-songwriter being compared to Buckley's. The pair's interaction warrants a short aside. Wainwright never met Buckley, but for a while they circled the same clubs in New York. (Buckley drowned in Memphis in May 1997, and the song 'Memphis Skyline' is obliquely in his memory.) According to Lake, Wainwright sent his demo cassette to the managers of Sin-é, an East Village club in St Mark's Place, three times, only to be rejected three times. As Lake comments, they already had a resident singer-songwriter in the shape of Buckley, who released the EP *Live at Sin-é* in November 1993. Therefore the rejection was unlikely to be anything personal against Wainwright, but he felt slighted nonetheless (Lake, 2009: 74).[2]

Shortly following this experience, Wainwright returned to Montreal and the Café Sarajevo on Clark Street, a small bar and restaurant that featured music in the evenings. His music and performances proved popular at this venue, but frequent moves between Montreal and New York City prevented him from being physically part of a music scene.

When Loudon passed his demo cassette to Van Dyke Parks in 1995, in a sense Wainwright inserted himself into an existing Los Angeles music scene, in respect of his contract with DreamWorks.[3] In January 1996, Rufus performed a live showcase evening for DreamWorks at Club Soda (Avenue du Parc, Montreal). Representatives from the LA-based DreamWorks company travelled to hear Wainwright in Montreal, suggesting that despite his frequent changes of location, he – and they – considered the Canadian city to be his home turf. Additionally, Wainwright's family were able to attend his performance in Montreal, which boosted his confidence (Lake, 2009: 84). Club Soda was a more formal, cabaret-style venue than Cafe Sarajevo, and Wainwright began his evening with his pop songs, before "moving into the parlour with a Schubert song and the wish that those who had seen him at his intimate cafe shows would now follow him to his inevitable stadium rock performances" (*ibid.*: 85).

By March 1996, Wainwright had moved back to New York City, and begun a residency at Fez, which was a tiny (130 capacity) basement club under Time Café on the corner of Great Jones and Lafayette Street near Broadway in Lower Manhattan. The club was seven blocks away from the old Gaslight club that had helped Loudon find fame twenty years earlier. Soon after this spell in New York (according to Lake, during this period he passed the "New York trial"), he moved to Los Angeles to record his first, self-titled, album. He stayed in the old Hollywood-style hotel, Chateau Marmont, with members of the Los Angeles "scene" – a group of similarly aged actors, musicians and writers, living the "LA lifestyle" with friend and contemporary Teddy Thompson (*ibid.*: 113). In 1999 he moved into the Chelsea Hotel on 23rd Street, New York City, a place with decades of popular music history. Wainwright seems happy to place himself in this lineage, claiming that "one day there's definitely going to be a plaque on the front of the hotel that says 'Rufus Wainwright lived here, for a while'" (Scott, 2005: 25:20).[4] He wrote most of the material for *Poses* while living in this hotel, and even bought a New York apartment in Gramercy Park (Patalono, 2013). And yet, after six months, he moved back to Canada into a self-contained apartment in his mother's house, and divided his time between the East and West Coasts of North America. Here he began recording *Poses* with Pierre Marchand – an album that would be partly recorded in Canada, partly in New York City with Alex Gifford of the Propellerheads, and partly in Los Angeles. Wainwright described the following albums (*Want One*, 2003 and *Want Two*, 2004) as his "multi-city, multi-coastal album[s]", but as Lake observes, "in truth *Poses* had been recorded in much the same way" (2009: 174). 'Going to a Town', one of the first songs he wrote for his next album *Release the Stars*, overtly displayed his love-hate relationship with America, the country he had accepted as his home for so many years but governed (in the Bush era) by a politician and a party with whom he strongly disagreed (discussed in Chapter 3). "I'm so tired of you, America", the lyrics state. He moved to Berlin to record *Release the Stars*. He continued to express an awareness of place in performance on tour, where he frequently dressed in locally appropriate outfits and alluded to local history in his spoken introductions (dressing as Robin Hood in Nottingham, UK, and speaking at length about local figurehead Jane Austen in Bath, UK). Three years later, *All Days Are Nights: Songs for Lulu* was a song cycle for solo voice and piano, recorded in his homeland of Canada. Finally, Wainwright headed back to New York City where he wrote and recorded 2012's *Out of the Game*. By the time of his wedding to Jörn in the summer of 2012, they had made Long Island in New York State their home – despite Wainwright's bolt holes in Montreal and New York City. The frequent moves he made between different parts of the US and Canada, as well as Europe, indicate a willingness to embrace the nomadic lifestyle of a musician, and suggest a reason for his inability to fit into a contemporary scene. The multiple stylistic influences I have discussed in previous chapters can arguably be linked to his mobility as a popular musician, as well as his aesthetic leanings towards art music. Wainwright does not conform to a geographically and temporally located scene as defined by Cohen.

Regional Styles

Regional style can be heard in two ways: either through adoption of an identifiable regional accent, or through development and repetition of a style associated with a region, which does not represent it musically or verbally. Examples of the former include the clear Cockney (working-class London) accents heard in the 1990s Britpop movement (in, for example, Blur's 1994 single 'Girls and Boys' from the album *Parklife*), the strong Welsh accent in Cerys Matthews's lead vocals in Catatonia (active from 1995–2001), and Wainwright's frequent use of European languages in his songs. Examples of the latter regional style include the Merseybeat style of the 1960s, and the 1960s–80s Northern Soul movement in the United Kingdom.[5] In *Decline, Renewal and the City*, Cohen draws a link between the distinctive 1960s Merseybeat sound of the Beatles and others, and its city of origin, Liverpool. This guitar-based sound with emphasis on melody and vocal harmonies has no direct association with Liverpool and the Mersey, but through its association with the area comes under my categorization of regional style.[6] Wainwright's 'Greek Song' discussed in Chapter 3, where he "collaps[es] a number of Others into an amalgam of difference with no regard to actual Greek music" (Jones 2002: 104) also falls into this category.

An instance of Wainwright's relation to regional style is the fourth track on *Want Two*, 'The Art Teacher'. The song is influenced by Philip Glass's minimalism, with a piano backdrop constructed from a repetitive and constantly moving melodic cell. The parts move slowly, usually by step, creating a shifting harmony over the repetitive rhythm. Marius de Vries, who produced both the *Want* albums and later mixed *Release the Stars*, explained that Wainwright was inspired to mimic Glass's style after seeing the annual Free Tibet charity concert in 1996, held in New York with Glass as artistic director (Scott, 2005). Lake suggests that Wainwright imitated Glass's style in order to show that his interest in classical music extended further than nineteenth-century operatic composers (2009: 199). Wainwright performed at the concert in 2003.

Philip Glass can be firmly connected with New York. After his youth in Baltimore, he spent five years studying at the Juilliard School in New York. A two-year composer-in-residence in Pittsburgh and a short period studying composition with Nadia Boulanger in France followed (Potter, 2000: 254), but in 1967 Glass returned to New York City. By this point he had honed his compositional style, and he set about employing an ensemble to perform his works.[7]

'The Art Teacher' begins with four bars of minimalist piano introduction, featuring continuous quavers that alternate between the notes of an Ebm/Gb chord.[8] The song is in simple verse form, consisting of five sung verses, and one contrasting instrumental verse (verse 4). Wainwright's first verse reflects on the protagonist's school days. Verses 2, 3 and 5 are extended with a refrain. The harmony slowly shifts as each piano part (left hand/right hand) moves incrementally, usually by little more than a tone. Each verse is in AAB form, consisting of three eight-bar phrases. Unlike most of Wainwright's songs, which are clearly autobiographical, it is unclear whether 'The Art Teacher' is told from a first-person standpoint or the perspective of a constructed fictional protagonist. The lyrics describe a school trip to an art gallery and further ambiguity is created when Wainwright sings "I was just a girl then", describing his/her childhood infatuation with the eponymous art teacher leading the trip. The harmonic ambiguity implied by the oscillating piano backdrop compounds the gender ambiguity suggested by the lyrics.

Table 4.1: 'The Art Teacher', song structure

Introduction	
Verse 1:	0:08
Verse 2:	0:35
Refrain:	1:02
Verse 3:	1:18
Refrain:	1:43
Horn solo:	1:54
Verse 4:	2:28
Verse 5:	3:01
Refrain:	3:33

Verses 2 and 3 are based on the same musical material, containing only surface melodic differences and syllable scanning. These verses both contain an additional refrain: verse 2 ends with two statements lamenting the necessary secrecy of the schoolgirl crush, and verse 3 with wordplay on the previous mention of the artist William Turner: "Never have I turned to any other man".

A contrasting horn solo follows, accompanied by a continuation of the repetitive piano accompaniment. Verse 4 is constructed of different melodic and harmonic material, and the lyrics reveal the subject matter to be the reflections of an adult woman on her youth. The twelve-bar structure of the previous verses is extended with a three-bar phrase. A full bar on each word "I own one" allows the listener time for reflection, giving time to consider that the protagonist may not be entirely convinced by her life choices: an interpretation highlighted by the ambiguity of lyrics and harmony discussed above.

Verse 5 is a resolution, both of the musical material (which returns to that of verses 1–3), and of the subject matter of the lyrics. The first two lines: "And here I am in this uniformish pantsuit sort of thing/Thinking of the art teacher" suggest that the protagonist has not been able to move on. The attire of a New York housewife traps her into a sartorial uniform, suggesting that despite the passage of time, she has not been able to progress from the social conformity of a school uniform. The final verse of the song contains an extended refrain, followed by three bars of piano interlude. The closing line of the verse, reiterating "I was just a girl then", and proclaiming that the protagonist has never loved another man since the art teacher, refutes her marriage to an "executive company head". In the final refrain, Wainwright reiterates this lyric and emotion twice, extending the melody and continuing the piano accompaniment for a further six bars, before ending with a rolled Gb6 chord. The finality of the harmonic conclusion in Gb major provides a musical answer to the questions posed in 'The Art Teacher' – the fictional protagonist did love the unnamed art teacher, and although she is unhappy with her marriage to the executive company head, she is happy in her reflections upon the incident. When recounting a class discussion of 'The Art Teacher', Roger Bourland of the University of California, Los Angeles, comments that a student recalled Wainwright stating that he was both himself and the constructed persona in the song. Bourland suggests that the line "I was just a girl then" "has double mea[n]ing for an effeminate man" (2006).

The art gallery provides cultural connotations of both high art and the setting of 1960s minimalist concerts, which often took place in art galleries. Wainwright sings about a specific visit to the Metropolitan Museum of Art in verse 1 – locating the events of the song to Fifth Avenue, Manhattan. 'The Art Teacher' is therefore a song that references place both musically (generically) and lyrically (specifically).

The specific location gives a clue to any listener who has visited that gallery and can conjure up the venue from memory, and suggests generic large display halls and galleries to listeners who have not visited the exact site. The song is therefore a good pivot point from which to move on to discussion of lyrical and musical representation in Wainwright's songs – the cultural connotations of the places evoked offer an additional interpretative layer.

Describing a named place in verbal content is a relatively straightforward method of evoking it in music, with famous examples being The Beatles' 'Penny Lane' and 'Strawberry Fields Forever' and The Kinks' 'Waterloo Sunset'. A selection of one or two lyrical references from each of Wainwright's studio-recorded albums provides an example of images and emotions conjured, alongside the autobiographical summary offered: 'Millbrook' (*Rufus Wainwright*); 'Poses' and 'California' (*Poses*); '14th Street' (*Want One*); 'Hometown Waltz', *Want Two*; 'Sanssouci' (*Release the Stars*); 'Who Are You New York?'(*All Days are Nights: Songs for Lulu*) and 'Montauk' (*Out of the Game*).

Yet, without lyrical reference, music can also evoke the spaces of a landscape or cityscape.[9] In Wainwright's music, 'Barcelona' and 'California' are examples. However, representations of place and space are not mutually exclusive, as can be seen in an in-depth analysis of 'Candles', using musical, lyrical and proxemic vocal analytical methods to evaluate the musical evocation of place and the use of virtual and physical space.

Many of Wainwright's song lyrics that make specific reference to place combine these allusions with biographical portraits. "The boys and girls of Millbrook/Are on a train from New York … Deep in the heart of Dutchess County" informs listeners about his days at the eponymous private boarding school in upstate New York ('Millbrook', *Rufus Wainwright*). *Poses* contains several lyrical and musical depictions of place: while lamenting his developing drug dependency on the title track, Wainwright sings "I'm drunk and wearing flip-flops on Fifth Avenue"; while the fifth track 'California' is directly addressed to the state, verbally painting a caricatured picture of Los Angeles stereotypes with lyrics such as "California, You're such a wonder that I think I'll stay in bed … Life is the longest death in California". After his decline into drug addiction and an ensuing spell in rehab, the *Want* albums marked Wainwright's reemergence into the popular music world. '14th Street', from *Want One*, refers specifically to a major street and cross-street in New York City, citing a triumphant homecoming to this adopted place of residence in no uncertain terms: "I'm coming back home tomorrow/to 14th Street where I won't hurry". In the commentary accompanying the albums, Wainwright himself states that "I actually wrote this song right … after I had shut down the shop for a while just to get the house in order, and this my return song … coming back to New York triumphant."[10] Beside 'The Art Teacher', *Want Two*'s 'Hometown Waltz' alludes to Wainwright's complex emotional attachment to Montreal, where he spent much of his youth. By describing the city as his "hometown", he underscores his sense of belonging – but this is sabotaged by lyrics such as: "You may ask why I want to torch my hometown … On Ontario Street". *Release the Stars* features 'Sansoucci', which evokes the former royal palace (now tourist destination) of King Frederick the Great.

The palace was his summer home in Berlin, and the name translates literally as "without care". An alternative reading of the song's title (because the lyrics are ambiguous) is that Wainwright refers to the nightclub owned in the 1930s by society dancers Vernon and Irene Castle. "Who will be at Sansoucci tonight?", he sings. The opening song on *All Days are Nights/Songs for Lulu* asks 'Who Are You New York?', with the anonymous protagonist singing about seeing "you" in various New York locations, including Grand Central Station, Madison Square Gardens and the Empire State Building. As discussed in Chapter 5, in *Out of the Game*'s 'Montauk', Wainwright sings about the domestic setting and chores enjoyed by Viva's "two dads" in the family home on Long Island.[11]

Lyrical depictions of places can be enriched by musical portrayals of space. Some of the previously mentioned songs are characterized geographically both in straightforward lyrical terms (Krims's "blunt tool"), and in nonverbal depictions of landscape. 'Barcelona', for example, contains both lyrical references to specific places evoking loneliness and disease ("today I felt a chill in my apartment's coolest place ... don't think there's pain in Barcelona"), and bare musical guitar phrases accompanying Wainwright's melancholic singing voice, which creates a soundscape of desolation and isolation. Another example of the joint lyrical and musical characterization of landscape takes place in 'California', in which lazy, long and wide melodies and accompanying backdrop of piano, guitar and rolling drum beat create an image that duplicates the long and wide roads and landscape of the West Coast.[12] Justin Williams has identified Los Angeles as a car-centric city to be driven in, stating that the city's "development as an automobile-dependent region, simultaneously dense and sprawling, undoubtedly bestowed a unique effect on various social and cultural realms" (2010: 163). Williams's idea is reinforced by Lake's opinion that 'California' "turned the ennui of [RW's] months of monotonous sun-filled days watching *The Golden Girls* on television and waiting to go to the studios of Los Angeles into a catchy, top-down and driving radio-friendly bounce" (2009: 121).[13]

'Candles'

My final example of the musical evocation of space is the concluding song on 2012's *Out of the Game*. According to Wainwright, 'Candles' is about trying to light a candle in memory of his mother after her death. Three churches in the New York environs could not provide them, which is reflected in the three verses which each repeat "the churches had run out of candles". The recorded track is in contrasting verse-chorus form, with a structure as follows:

Table 4.2: 'Candles', song structure

Instrumental Introduction (0:00–0:17)
Verse 1 (0:18–0:52)
Chorus (0:53–1:26)
Verse 2 (1:26–1:59)
Chorus (2:00–2:34)
Interlude: Instrumental and Backing Vocals (2:34–3:06)
Verse 3 (3:07–3:41)
Chorus (3:42–4:14)
Chorus (4:15–4:56)
Interlude 2: Instrumental and Backing Vocals (4:57–5:31)
Chorus (5:32–6:11)
Bagpipe Solo and Instrumental Fade-out (6:12–7:42)

'Candles' begins with four bars of acoustic guitar strumming quavers in a 4/4 metre, subdivided into 3+3+2 (reflected in the note beaming in Figure 4.1). This creates an acoustic, folk-like, sound world that pays a musical homage to Kate's performance tradition. The slow, steady pulse (at around crotchet = 56, with each quaver demarcated and emphasis on the first quaver of each subdivision) means that the duration of each line of lyrics is four bars. Sixteen-bar blocks of musical material therefore cover four lines of lyrics, or an entire verse or chorus. In the first half of the song, each verse segues straight into a chorus (with repeated basic melodic/harmonic material, but slowly building texture and instrumentation, labelled as numbered verse/chorus blocks).

Verse/chorus block 1 leads directly into verse/chorus block 2, which is followed by an eight-bar instrumental interlude with the addition of wordless backing vocals (sung by Loudon, Martha, Lucy Roche, Sloan Wainwright, Jenni Muldaur and Chaim Tannenbaum). The presence of many members of the extended Wainwright family indicates a large-scale remembrance of Kate, and suggests a warming of relations between Rufus and Loudon. Piano and synthesizer become more audible at this point. The addition of synthesizer does not disturb the sound world, for it is set to resemble an acoustic harmonica or similar, and serves to build up the instrumental texture. A snare drum (played by David Budge) joins on the upbeat to verse/chorus block 3, building the folk references by referencing the rhythm and timbre of a Scotch snap. Verse 3 is important for the subject matter of the song, for up to this point it has been a lament and reflection on loss and searching. According to the song, Wainwright eventually located a candle for Kate in Paris's Notre Dame cathedral, and the mood of the lyrical content reflects this. Figure 4.1 shows more positive lyrics, as well as depicting the melodic and harmonic structure heard in each verse/chorus block. The timings shown are a notated version of my reading of the basic rhythmic framework. Wainwright adds musical and emotional interpretation by adding rubato within the context of the beat or the bar ("micro-rubato"), or by emphasizing upper notes. My notation shows the basic structure, rather than a quantization of interpretations in specific recordings or performances. However, despite the clear programme behind 'Candles' expressed in interviews and elsewhere (for example in Swift, 2012), the lyrics of the song do not refer to identified places.

Figure 4.1: 'Candles', verse/chorus block 3, transcription KW

The second half of the song features two further repetitions of the chorus. Chorus 3 segues directly into chorus 4. He delays the final line, by pausing on the following italicized syllables: "the *chur*ches have *run* out of *cand*les." Chorus 4 is followed by a second instrumental/backing vocals interlude, this time with the addition (continuation) of snare. Wainwright repeats the chorus one final time, with the same caesuras. The track ends with a twenty-bar bagpipe solo entering over his final sung note, and an instrumental fade-out to silence.

Proxemics

Application of the proxemic method of analysis to 'Candles' is enlightening when considering the evocation of space in a vocal performance. The proxemic method is an analysis of space in recorded vocals developed by Allan Moore, Patricia Schmidt and Ruth Dockwray after anthropologist Edward T.

Hall's designation of zones of spatial interaction between people. Hall categorized interactions into four zones: intimate, personal, social and public, each of which had a close and far phase (1963, 1966, 1969). Hall's categories included aspects of social interaction comprising posture, physical groupings of people, thermal and olfactory realizations of close interactions, and the voice loudness scale (Hall, 1963: 1006–1007). The latter factor is of relevance to this argument, as Hall defines the vocal sounds and timbre necessary for conversation in each zone.

Moore *et al.* applied Hall's zones to recorded music in this way:

> Two basic determining elements of [Hall's] characterization of each zone, and their component qualities, remain fundamental in our adaptation: the concept of personal space, which is individualized and surrounds a person; and the concept of interpersonal distance, which refers to the related distance between two persons. In the context of recorded song, we refer to the personal space of the listener, though a sense of the persona's personal space is also integral to any characterization of its relationship to the environment, while our understanding of interpersonal distance theorizes a distance between the listener's perceptual position and the position of the song's persona, as modified by its (personic) environment. (2009: 99)

For each zone, the authors identified features of the distance between the song's persona and the listener, the relationship between the persona and the musical environment, and the articulation of persona (referring to lyrical content, timbral quality of voice and non-vocal sounds).[14] Essentially, the intimacy of a recorded lead vocal has very little to do with the dynamic at which the vocal is heard: in the studio, a whisper can be turned up to the volume of a shout, without losing any of its characteristic vocal qualities. Serge Lacasse suggested a definition for the quality of a singer's voice: "paralinguistic features, such as the performer's distinct timbre, the gestural attitude he/she adopts while singing, etc." (2000: 20). Because studio techniques are advanced in the twenty-first century, we must assume that any non-singing sounds left in the mix (breaths, coughs etc.) are done so with intent, in order to produce an intimate vocal that enables the listener to form a close relationship with the singer.

Rufus Wainwright's recorded vocal performance (the "track") of 'Candles' can be placed in the intimate proxemic zone. His vocal is recorded at a close range, with an unforced, intimate tonal quality. The close-mic technique means that Wainwright does not have to strain his voice, and the timbral sound created here is resonant and rich. The lead vocal sounds close to the listener – unlike the instrumental accompaniment and backing vocals, which are distant (to the rear of the sound-box, to utilize a methodology explained and developed further in Chapter 5). In addition, the paralingual sounds – in this case, inhalations of breath – are clearly audible, and serve to reinforce the intimacy of the recorded performance, and to clearly demarcate phrase shape. These clearly audible breaths are marked with phrase marks/commas on Figure 4.1.

'Candles', live performance

In addition, the large intervals of the melody, and the slow-moving pitches, evoke music written for performance in a large space, for they resonate effectively in such venues. In live performance, Wainwright frequently performs 'Candles' a capella (unaccompanied), without amplification, to allow his natural singing voice to fill his performance venue. On 24 July 2011, the final night of the House of Rufus Royal Opera House (Covent Garden, London) residency, news had just broken of singer Amy Winehouse's death. As a final encore, Wainwright dedicated an unaccompanied, acoustic version of 'Candles' to Winehouse. Wainwright requested silence from his audience, which created an aura of respect and reverence for the song, the deceased Winehouse, and the performance venue.[15] This performance served a dual purpose: as well as providing an emotional and heartfelt tribute, the spotlight on the unaccompanied singer on the enormous Royal Opera House stage emphasized the size of the venue in which he was performing. Singing acoustically encouraged him to project his voice in a way that is not demanded by studio recordings.

Moore *et al.*'s proxemic analysis is intended for recorded tracks. Here, however, it is useful to apply and adapt the methodology to Wainwright's live performance of the same song. This case study provides an example of how his music is shaped by performance space. Rufus Wainwright's performance of 'Candles' to a live audience on 24 July 2011 is markedly different to the recorded track released on *Out of the Game*. Wainwright sang entirely unaccompanied, commanding the stage. The sheer volume and projection of his voice ensured that attention was focused on him. In this unaccompanied context, the structure of the song was changed slightly: he proceeded directly through the text, with no repetitions other than alternating the verse and chorus, and no instrumental interludes (despite both vocal performances being at similar speeds, the shortened lyrical content of the latter ensured that his live performance lasted around three minutes, around half the duration of the studio version). To ensure projection and filling the internal space of the Royal Opera House, Wainwright alternated between a speech quality and a musical-theatre style belting voice (heard on the upper notes: "run" is emphasized in each verse and chorus, as is "lit" in verse 3). This emphasis is greater than that heard in the recorded track. This is not simply a dynamic shift, as in the latter; the timbral quality of his voice changes. In performance, Wainwright clearly tilted his head back to project and articulate these upper notes.[16] The transition between each type of voice was smooth because he uses lots of twang/nasal characteristics throughout. No paralinguistic sounds can be heard – this is a much more direct and focused sound than the intimate vocal quality and small acoustic space implied on *Out of the Game*. The unaccompanied performance means that a proxemic reading is complex; the vocals cannot be measured in relation to their backing vocals and instruments. By performing without amplification, recording distance from the microphone cannot be measured. However, the popularity of the House of Rufus residency, and the cultural power that afforded a tribute to singer Amy Winehouse, mean that many bootleg recordings exist. Members of the audience documented the performance on smartphones and pocket devices, and videos can be found online with a simple internet search.[17] In this performance, 'Candles' can be placed in the public proxemic zone, as his vocal quality is full and loud, no vocal sounds are heard, and the vocals address a large audience.

Perhaps the most interesting aspect of Wainwright's residency at the Royal Opera House, though, is his awareness of the prestige afforded his music through performances in a venue of such cultural worth. The following section addresses cultural connotations of performance venues for Wainwright and his audiences, and explains the increasing number of performances he undertakes in art music venues.

Performing/Listening Spaces

The above analysis of 'Candles' showed how the components of the song (melodic structure, harmony, form and tempo) suggest that it is intended for a large listening space. However, the proxemic reading of the recorded track implies a much more intimate listening environment, and the performance at the Royal Opera House on 24 July 2011 shows how the song can be modified to fit a public proxemic zone – implying a much larger performance and listening space.

I have noted elsewhere the cultural connotations of performance spaces, and the appropriation of reception styles by performing music in spaces intended for different styles (Williams, 2012a). A similar effect can be seen in Rufus Wainwright's performance trajectory throughout his career: from Montreal coffee shops and folk festivals with his mother and aunt in the late 1970s; to small nightclubs in the first years of his solo performing career in the 1990s; to supporting the Barenaked Ladies and Tori Amos in rock stadia

(Lake, 2009: 116); to large rock festivals (for example, Wainwright has frequently performed at Toronto's Luminato Festival, and played at the Pyramid Stage at Glastonbury in 2013, along with numerous other appearances at large-scale music festivals in recent years) and venues predominantly associated with art music in the 2000s.[18]

The music and lyrical allusions to opera in songs discussed in Chapter 3 provide cultural connotations of opera houses. Wainwright's references to Franz Schubert provide associations with intimate domestic spaces such as the parlour to audiences familiar with performance trends in classical music: Schubert songs were first performed in (and is arguably most suited to) the parlour. Lake's account of Wainwright's showcase performance at Club Soda reinforces this, recounting that after performing several numbers from his popular catalogue, 'Rufus ... moved into the parlour with a Schubert song' (*ibid.*: 85).

An important event to consider is Wainwright's 2006 recreation of Judy Garland's iconic 1961 Carnegie Hall concert. Wainwright insisted that it was not an imitation, but a way of paying homage and proving himself on a culturally respected musical stage. The *Rufus! Rufus! Rufus! Does Judy! Judy! Judy!* shows were doubly important for Wainwright's position as a gay singer-songwriter. First, Judy Garland is one of the old stars of showbusiness, and her 1961 performance of twenty-six standards from the American songbook is culturally revered.[19] In addition, Garland has been appropriated as an icon of the gay community: something that started with her portrayal of Dorothy in the 1939 film version of *The Wizard of Oz*, and continued into her later life – heightened by her associations with musical theatre and her tendency to publicly play out the trials of her life.[20] Richard Dyer explains the ways in which "various aspects of [Garland's] image spoke to different elements within male gay subcultures" (1986: 138). He locates 1950 as the point in which her image and career became an important focus for gay culture. In that year she was dropped by Metro-Goldwyn-Mayer (MGM), and her clean-cut "preppy" image and singing style (*ibid.*: 158) began to disintegrate. The vocal inadequacies in the last stages of Garland's life are audible on the recording of her 1961 concert. In this respect, a parallel can be drawn with the diva Maria Callas. Lake (2009: 216–41) and Schwandt (2010: 65–72) evaluate the cultural implications of Wainwright reproducing Garland's performance from his position as an openly homosexual musician.[21]

In February 2007, Wainwright repeated the performance at London's Palladium Theatre. This venue has important associations for Judy Garland's career: it was the site of her first UK performance in 1951; she performed there alongside The Beatles to great acclaim in 1964; it was the venue of her debut performance with her daughter Liza Minnelli in 1964; and she performs many songs on the Palladium stage in her last film *I Could Go on Singing* (1964).

The London Palladium performance was recorded and released as a DVD (2007). The editing of *Rufus! Rufus! Rufus! Does Judy! Judy! Judy! Live from the London Palladium* shows awareness of the venue, and of the performance as a stage show. At the opening of the DVD, the camera pans the Palladium, and zooms in on the stage, clearly illustrating that this is a filmed performance, rather than falsifying "realism". A parallel can be seen in opera DVDs, in which the aim is usually to maintain a live aesthetic, as Carlo Cenciarelli has pointed out (2013: 204). He writes:

> In spite of the video's potential to extricate the work from the broader social and cultural contexts of opera-going, or rather precisely because of that, its paratexts typically work hard to contextualise the performance, dedicating some screen time to the venue's exteriors and interiors. Large's video of the 1983 [*Don Carlo*] performance at the MET provides a typical example. In a way characteristic of the MET telecasts of the time, the video starts with an external shot of the opera house, centrally framed on its famous façade. In front of the wall of glass, with its five soaring arches, the fountain reflects the electric lights of the Lincoln Center ... Soon the camera starts a slow zoom into the building, closing in on a crystal chandelier visible through the façade ... For a moment, the camera lingers on the staircase ... Then, through another cross-fade, we find ourselves in the auditorium, where patrons are starting to sit down. (*Ibid.*: 217)

The focus on the venue in Wainwright's DVD shows both an awareness of the cultural significance of the London Palladium, and the framing devices that suggest *Rufus! Rufus! Rufus! Does Judy! Judy! Judy!* can be considered alongside the opera DVDs with which it has parallels.

5 The Voice

Rufus Wainwright's voice is characterful, expressing his own lived experiences, showing the musical influences of classical, opera, popular music, folk and musical theatre. His voice is capable of being reedy and rich, nasal and full-throated, and is equally suited to the popular music stage, the opera hall, or Broadway. He is able to slide smoothly through a warm tenor, head voice, head voice into falsetto, and a true falsetto, enabling a range of vocalized personas. Rufus himself has referred to his "immense [vocal] range" (Scott, 2009: 26:28). Singers, writers and scholars alike have commented upon the multifarious qualities of his voice. Janis Kelly, who sang the title role in *Prima Donna*, commented upon Rufus Wainwright's "great voice". "He can actually sing higher than a lot of tenors", she said, "and has fantastic breath control. And it's his own unique sound" (2013). As Matthew J. Jones comments: "The immensity of Wainwright's voice imbues it with physicality beyond that of a mere instrument in the mix; it becomes the central figure in the unfolding drama of ... each individual song" (2002: 81).

Wainwright's voice gets more prominent in the recorded mix of his studio albums as time progresses – something that can be attributed both to a developing compositional style that showcases his voice, and to his choice of producers. Additionally, the increasing dominance of his voice reflects his increasingly overblown and voracious ego. Here, "ego" is used to mean both the popular understanding of the term, a focus on the self, arrogance or conceit – and the Freudian psychoanalytical meaning of the term, the development of a personal identity, or sense of self. "Ego" also refers to the autobiographical tendency of his songs.

Rufus Wainwright's burgeoning ego (in all these senses) is reflected in the dedications of each of his albums, which provide another facet to his life story and authorial role. Analysis of his recorded sound, borrowing from Ruth Dockwray and Allan Moore's sound-box methodology (Moore, 2010; Dockwray and Moore, 2010), shows that Wainwright's growing ego is reflected by an increasingly voice-dominated composition and recording style. This is a spatial realization of the sonic placement of components of the mix (the "stereo image"). These components are mapped onto a four-dimensional box, with the axes respectively representing laterality, register, prominence and temporal continuity.[1]

The sound-box analyses and narration of biography are enhanced by acknowledging the producers who were used to make each subsequent album. It also appears that as Rufus Wainwright became more comfortable with his place in the popular music world, he exerted a more tangible authorial role on his music. In this way, he exerted a growing Freudian sense of ego.

Rufus Wainwright
When Rufus Wainwright signed with DreamWorks Records in 1998, his contract allowed him complete freedom over arrangements and orchestral forces, a clause he used fully on his first album (produced by Van Dyke Parks). The complex musical and production aesthetic that Van Dyke Parks favoured at the time is evident on *Rufus Wainwright*, which featured combinations of ten different musicians, who were often multi-tracked on different instruments and vocals. The most instrumentally busy tracks, 'Foolish Love', 'In My Arms' and 'Sally Ann', feature six instrumentalists/vocalists. Thirty-nine instruments (including vocals and backing vocals) are heard on the album, and Van Dyke Parks and Randy Brion provide arrangements and conduct.

Dockwray and Moore's sound-box is a useful tool for assessing the prominence of the voice in recorded song. As Moore writes,

> the sound box acts as a virtual space 'enclosure' for consideration of sound sources. This model aims to plot the perceived sound world of a recording three-dimensionally, in terms of the width of the stereo image, proximity of the various elements to the listener, and the comparative pitch and register of the various sound sources. (Moore, 2010: 146–47).[2]

Dockwray and Moore identify four common kinds of stereo imaging: the "clustered mix", in which the three key sounds of bass guitar, snare drum and lead vocals are all centrally placed; the "triangular mix", in which these key elements form any shape of triangle; the "dynamic mix", where there is some level of movement in sound sources; and the "diagonal mix", where the vocals, bass and snare are placed on a diagonal sonic line, with extraneous instruments placed to either side (Dockwray and Moore, 2010: 186).

'Danny Boy'

The second song featured on *Rufus Wainwright*, 'Danny Boy', is autobiographical, documenting Rufus's early infatuation with a straight man named Danny (Lake, 2009: 72).[3] My chosen extract is the first two sung lines, after an instrumental introduction. The lyrics at this point state: "Your skin is cold/but the sun shines within your hold".

A simplicity and naïvety can be heard, alongside a youthful rawness in Wainwright's voice. A Barthesian reading of this recording suggests that significance lies *between* the pheno-song and the geno-song. The elusive *grain* of Wainwright's singing voice provides meaning beyond these coded methods. This youth and childlike naïvety (Wainwright was twenty-five years old when his debut album was recorded) are reflected in the dedication, which simply reads: "This record is dedicated to my grandparents, whom I hope are watching from the best seats in the sky."

Figure 5.1: 'Danny Boy', 0:19–0:40, sound-box analysis KW

Figure 5.1 is a sound-box analysis for the chosen extract. The excerpt begins with a repetitive, rolling accompaniment figure, played on keyboard instruments, reinforced by bass and baritone guitar. These backgrounds are marginally quieter than the voice, and placed at equidistant points around the periphery of the stereo field (bass guitar to the left, piano at the back right, and baritone guitar to the right). Although only marginally louder than the accompanying instruments, the voice is placed at the front centre of the stereo field (represented in the sound-box diagram by a picture of Wainwright inside a circle – a modification of Moore *et al.*'s unidentified open mouths). The rhythmic contours of the background figure are accented throughout with soft bass drum hits, but the drums' presence is announced forcibly with a cymbal crash at 0:41 on the recorded track (0:23 of the selected extract), with the positioning at the back left of the stereo field completing the encirclement of Wainwright's voice.

The piano image in the sound-box diagram also represents a tack piano (which is prepared to sound uncared for, like a misused music-hall piano, playing music in the "honky-tonk" style), optigan and S-6 synthesizer. Later in the track, Randy Brion's horn arrangement enters, and the song crescendos to a peak of emotional intensity. The increase in volume is manipulated to ensure that the voice retains its spatial placement in the mix, and is not swamped by the addition of brass instruments. 'Danny Boy' falls into the category Dockwray and Moore (2010) designate as a "cluster mix", where all the musical elements are clustered into a narrow aural space in the centre of the sound-box. In general, the mix of this song is uniform, with the instruments and voice sounding as one aural conglomerate.

Poses
2001's *Poses* was a conscious attempt to make a more accessible record in order to attract a larger commercial audience. Musically, Rufus simplified his piano parts from those featured on *Rufus Wainwright* and used electronica, beats and loops in an attempt to make his style more popular. During the recording and release of his second album, Rufus moved into the famously "rock and roll" Chelsea Hotel on Fifth Avenue in New York, and embraced the clichéd and mythologized pop-star lifestyle. Whilst enjoying the moderate success and fame that accompanied his album sales and live performances, his dependence on drugs and alcohol escalated. In particular, he became seriously addicted to crystal meth (methamphetamine). The title track, featured third on the album, documents this period – essentially, Rufus Wainwright was writing and behaving himself into the pop-star lineage.

Posing, or the pose(u)r, can be interpreted in a number of ways. Lake suggests that Rufus used the term as a synonym for "roles", creating a fictional protagonist that can simply be abandoned if life becomes difficult or dangerous (2009: 143). Jones offers another reading: that the "poses" in question are adopted nineteenth-century personas, one of which is the French *flâneur* (the subject of a study in the early twentieth century by Walter Benjamin), and another of which, Jones suggests, is the Wildean dandy of the English late 1800s (2002: 32–33).

In *The Saturated Self* (1991), Kenneth J. Gergen argues that developments in technology over the previous decades have resulted in a "saturated sense of self". He identifies a nineteenth-century romantic sense of self as "one that attributes to each person characteristics of personal depth: passion, soul, creativity and moral fiber" (1991: 6). Throughout the increasingly technologically connected and yet socially detached twentieth century, he argues, romanticism gave way to modernism. "For modernists the chief characteristics of the self reside not in the domain of depth, but rather in our ability to reason – in our beliefs, opinions and conscious intentions" (*ibid.*). Furthermore, as the century progressed, people began to develop multiple selves for the different aspects of contemporary life: a persona for long-distance telephone calls, one for emails, one for social networking, and so on. Gergen defines this process as "multiphrenia", or a splitting of the individual into a multiplicity of identities (*ibid.*: 73). Multiphrenia is an apt description of Rufus Wainwright's creation and adoption of a number of "poses", each time playing a role that can be discarded at any given time.

'Poses'

'Poses' is a tango, accompanied by acoustic piano, strings, oboe and drum-kit. The song is structured in eight four-line blocks, with the pattern of three verses followed by a contrasting chorus repeated twice. The chosen extract for analysis is verse 5.

Figure 5.2: 'Poses', 2:42–3:04, sound-box analysis KW

My sound-box analysis (Figure 5.2) is taken from the middle of this extract. Acoustic piano can be heard on both sides of the stereo field: left-hand playing an arpeggiated tango rhythm (doubled by *arco* cello, on the right), and a right-hand piano counter-melody (higher pitched, and positioned to the right of the stereo field). A violin counter-melody can be heard to the left of the stereo field. Percussion can be heard in the track (not pictured on analysis): a bass drum can be heard at the back of the sound-box, and tom-toms above the bass drum. An occasional triangle accent can be heard to the far left.

Backing vocals join from 2:48 on the recorded track (0:06 of the extract), positioned behind the lead vocal, and portrayed by a small picture (the image is of Rufus Wainwright, but here the backing vocals are sung by Martha). As can be seen from Figure 5.2 the lead voice is higher in the mix than on the first album – aurally depicting his increasing ego and adopted pop-star personality.[4] Jones comments on the placement of lead and backing vocals in the mix:

> The placement of backing vocals, provided by Wainwright's sibling Martha, at the 'bottom' of the mix suggests a devaluing of both the contributions of women to his art and, more generally, those of

others. Kept from finishing a complete word until the final iteration of the chorus, the backing vocals conduct the listener's attention back to Wainwright's voice, and by association, Wainwright himself. (2002: 61–62)

Jones's comment underscores my belief that Wainwright's increasing confidence in his sense of self is manifested musically. A plethora of producers are credited: Pierre Marchand, Ethan Johns, Damian Legassic, Greg Wells, and Alex Gifford of the British group The Propellorheads, with Waronker again as executive producer. This extract is an example of a "diagonal mix", with the main instruments (piano, cello, percussion and vocals) in a diagonal line within the sound-box, with extraneous instruments placed to either side. Despite the busyness of the track, though, Wainwright's voice is definitively at the forefront.

The album's dedication to the group of friends with whom he "experienced [his] second childhood" (Scott, 2005: 25:40) also reflects the fun-chasing nature of the period with a series of memories and in-jokes:

This record is dedicated to Zaldy, Michael and Walt, who reminded me that it's OK to say "Fabulous", OK to skip school, and OK to make out with someone at the bar. Any bar. "Long live the duck!"

Want One/Want Two

Wainwright had already begun work on a third album with producer Marius de Vries when he checked into rehabilitation in summer 2002, and continued writing during his recovery, eventually recording thirty tracks in an intense burst of creativity in January 2003. He titled the sessions *Want*, and they represent a return to and extension of the elaborate and complex style of his first album.[5]

From the beginning, the *Want* project illustrates a stronger musical grasp on the proceedings. The list of credits on *Want One* (released September 2003) is much simpler than the preceding albums, simply stating "Produced by Marius de Vries, and Executive Producer Lenny Waronker". But perhaps most tellingly, the dedication simply states: "This record is dedicated to me", paying tribute to his battle with drugs and rehabilitation, and to his increasing command of his own music and life. His inflating ego is characterized musically by such devices as the use of a bombastic tuba bass line in the opening 'Oh What a World', quotation of Ravel's 'Bolero' melody, and double and multi-tracking of his own voice. Rufus Wainwright's increasing ego as shown by the placement of his own voice in each subsequent album can be explained with a Freudian reading.[6]

Rufus Wainwright's ego (in the Freudian sense) can be heard clearly in the prominence of his voice in the recorded mix on *Want Two*. The songs are autobiographical (as mentioned earlier, he made a conscious effort to insert himself into a pop-star lineage). *Want Two* illustrates Rufus Wainwright's growing comfort with his sense of self and authorial role still further. Marius de Vries is listed as a producer alongside Rufus Wainwright as co-producer (on 'Old Whore's Diet') and as sole producer (on 'Hometown Waltz'). This is a clear shift towards Wainwright adopting more authorial control over his recorded output.

'Old Whore's Diet'

DreamWorks released *Want Two* in November 2004. The album is bookended by two songs that particularly foreground Wainwright's vocals. The text of the opening track, 'Agnus Dei', is entirely in Latin, based on the liturgical text. The voice enters a full minute and half after a string introduction, based on drones and Eastern European influences. The track grows to large orchestral proportions, and serves as an introduction for an album that continues to feature voice and orchestra heavily. Rufus's increasing confidence in himself can be heard in the prominence of his voice in 'Old Whore's Diet', the final track.[7] Wainwright's voice is foregrounded throughout the track, despite intricate instrumentation and guest vocals from Antony Hegarty of Antony and the Johnsons. The nine-minute song has only eleven lines of lyrical text, which reinforces the fact that the *sound* of the voice is privileged over textual content. Johnson's voice is even more theatrical than Wainwright's, and the juxtaposition of the two voices and their extensive vibrato creates drama. The song's content refers to waking up in his house during his drug-dependent days, and finding that he had not filled his fridge and cupboards adequately. The 'Old Whore's Diet' is the breakfast he is forced to consume when his mind is elsewhere, although the term could equally refer to the cocktail of drugs he frequently consumed. Figure 5.3 shows my sound-box analysis of the opening section of this track, which feature Rufus Wainwright's vocals at the forefront, accompanied at a much lesser level by guitar.

Figure 5.3: 'Old Whore's Diet', 0:00–0:37, sound-box analysis KW

After a rubato, melismatic opening, the track moves into a laid-back rock beat, with backing vocals, melisma from Antony Hegarty, and more vocal input from Rufus. In *Want Two* the overblown nature of Wainwright's ego is manifested musically not only in the increasing dominance of his voice in the recorded mix as his studio-recorded career progresses, but in the inclusion on the album of such tracks as 'Gay Messiah'. In live and televised performances of this song, he routinely dressed in heavenly garb, descending from the sky on a crucifix. He claimed to have been sent as the Gay Messiah to save homosexual people the world over (Lake, 2009: 193). By this time, Rufus Wainwright had become more bombastic musically and in performance. According to Freud's psychoanalytical analysis, "the id is totally non-moral [and] the ego strives to be moral" (1995: 655). We see that Rufus Wainwright's ego is giving way to the inevitability of the id.

Release the Stars
Four pages of the *Release the Stars* CD liner booklet are devoted to Rufus wearing lederhosen, in an exaggeration of his exhibitionist and narcissistic tendencies. In another example of his growing confidence in his sense of self, the initials "RW" are embroidered onto the front of the lederhosen, and can be clearly detected. One of the images, for example, focuses on his torso, and shows his ring-encrusted fingers tucked into the waistband of his trousers, while the band over his chest bears his identifying initials. The album is dedicated to Kate McGarrigle: "This album is dedicated to my mother, who still whispers in my ear that I'm great."

Despite the enormous scale of the orchestration and numerous instrumentalists involved,[8] the production credits are simple. Rufus Wainwright asserted his authorial voice by producing *Release the Stars* himself, with Pet Shop Boy Neil Tennant as executive producer, and the only other production credit going to sound engineer Tom Schick. The album contains a second dedication, hidden within the liner notes. "Special thanks to Tom Schick", it says. "Thanks for encouraging me to produce it myself." By this point, Wainwright had progressed from using an external producer, via co-producing, to being the sole producer – emphasizing the increased control he had over his own music.

'Do I Disappoint You'

My chosen extract from the opening track 'Do I Disappoint You?' incorporates the instrumental opening and first two lines of text. Rufus's voice can be heard very high in the mix – again, over the layered textures and heavy orchestration of the accompaniment. The lyrics here suggest that Rufus Wainwright feels unworthy of the unnamed addressee's love, and that he feels like a superfluous extra to their life: "Do I disappoint you in just being human?/And not one of the elements that you can light your cigar on."

The orchestration and instrumentation, however, contradict the lyrics in their extravagance. The ever-increasing scale of production and prominence of his voice suggest that, musically, Rufus Wainwright is not disappointed in himself.

Figure 5.4: 'Do I Disappoint You?', 0:00–0:30, sound-box analysis KW

Figure 5.4 shows my sound-box analysis of this extract. A triangular mix forms the basis of the sound here, a modified version of Dockwray and Moore's three key elements (vocal, piano and percussion). The instrumental backing begins with a sustained didgeridoo note, which is soon joined by a rolling figure created from many instrumental components, including percussion (timpani, shaker and triangle), and piano percussion.[9] Wainwright's voice joins shortly afterwards, punctuated by ascending figures played by two flutes. The list of credits for this song is extensive: Rufus Wainwright is listed for vocals, piano and orchestral arrangements; Larry Mullins for shaker, triangle, glockenspiel, cymbals, cowbells, timpani, bells, bass drum, tambourine, vibes and piano percussion; Martha Wainwright for backing vocals; Neil Tennant for samples and loops, a string quintet, a twelve-piece brass section, and flute; and Marius de Vries and Jason Boshoff for programming. In this disjunction between the orchestral forces and the vocal placement with the subdued lyrics, it is again possible to see that the id overrides the ego.

All Days are Nights: Songs for Lulu
The creation and recording of *Release the Stars* marked a turbulent personal time in Rufus Wainwright's life. The period was characterized by a series

of positive and negative personal events. His next album, released in March 2010, reflected these personal sorrows and joys. *All Days are Nights: Songs for Lulu* was a melancholic sequence of songs for solo voice and piano (with hints of Robert Schumann's *Dichterliebe* and Franz Schubert's *Winterreise*). These art music concerns are furthered in the presentation of the album: it was engineered by Tom Schick for Decca, and again produced by Rufus Wainwright.[10]

'Martha'

The third track of the album is addressed to his sister. 'Martha' deals with the concerns of adult siblings caring for their aging, ill and estranged parents. The sparseness of the piano backdrop underlines the foregrounding of Rufus's voice (shown in my sound-box analysis of the opening in Figure 5.5). Using Dockwray and Moore's terminology, this is a "triangular mix", but the presence of only two musical elements demands a renaming, perhaps "linear mix".

Figure 5.5: 'Martha', 0:00–0:35, sound-box analysis KW

The dedication underscored Rufus's reflections on mortality and family at this time (as documented in many press interviews). On the front cover, he states "To Martha, the bright lady", while on the back, he lists:

> Thanks to all my family and friends
> Special thanks to Jörn for always rubbing my feet
> Special, special thanks to Kate for reminding me not to be afraid.
> See you in Montauk, Mom. X[11]

Out of the Game
The reference to Montauk in *All Days are Nights*' dedication has two possible interpretations. Montauk is a famous tourist destination in Long Island, New

York State, with several State parks within its boundaries. Montauk is also the "Wainwright family home". Jörn and Rufus extended their family unit in February 2011, when Lorca Cohen (daughter of Leonard) gave birth to a daughter fathered by Rufus, named Viva Katherine Wainwright Cohen.[12] 2012's *Out Of the Game* is dedicated to Viva ("Welcome to the ball!", the liner notes read), while several songs on the album are addressed to the Viva of the future.

'Montauk'

In 'Montauk', Rufus sings about "your dad" and "your other dad", hoping that one day Viva (who spent her childhood living with her mother in Los Angeles) will visit her fathers at home. *Out of the Game* is a homage to the 1970s style of singer-songwriter and recording, and is produced by retro producer Mark Ronson. In 2012 Wainwright commented on the factor that drew him to Ronson: "Mark's talent is that he actually makes the artists shine and come forth. He has always done his best work with vocalists – which essentially I am. It's all about the voice. On this record he's not allowed my voice to get lost in the process. It's at the front and centre" (Swift, 2012). The extract from 'Montauk' shown in the following sound-box analysis (Figure 5.6) occurs near the opening of the track, which is placed sixth of twelve songs on the album.

Again, the voice is very high in the mix, with an equal balance of synthesizer on a string pad (depicted as a MIDI keyboard) and rippling acoustic piano distant in the background (right hand plays sextuplet arpeggios, while the left hand marks out a crotchet pulse). A triangular mix can again be heard, but here it is helpful to envision a triangle laid on a horizontal axis, with the voice at the forefront, and the two backing sounds receding into the distance at equal points.

Figure 5.6: 'Montauk', 0:07–0:29, sound-box analysis KW

The additional reading of 'Montauk' that I wish to offer is that for New Yorkers, it is quite simply the end of the line. It is the final stop on the Long Island Railroad, and suggests that Rufus (and Jörn, and Viva) have reached their final destination and are content to settle down. By the increasing prominence of his own voice in the recorded mix of his studio records, it is possible to see that Rufus Wainwright has become more comfortable and confident with his musical style. It is possible to conflate these two readings, and see a shift from the ego to the id in the increasing prominence of his voice and growing domesticity of his lyrics.

Brief consideration of the vocal recording technique of a track from each album (sometimes the same track as considered for my sound-box analyses, and sometimes a different track for a clearer example) show how Wainwright's recorded vocals follow a similar proxemic trajectory to that illustrated by my series of sound-box analyses. (Proxemics are explained more fully in Chapter 4.)

'Baby' is featured sixth on *Rufus Wainwright*, and can be placed in the close intimate proxemic zone. In this zone, according to Moore *et al.*, the vocal sounds very close to the listener, and there is no intervening musical material. The rawness and depth of the vocal is enhanced by the proximity to the listener, and the accompanying piano and shimmering strings sound far from the voice. The vocal again adheres to proxemic criteria by including a number of clear non-vocal sounds (for example, gasped intakes of breath at 0:15, 0:19, 0:22 and 0:29 in the first two lines). The lyrical content, write Moore *et al.*, "suggests intimacy/physical contact and addressed interpersonal relationship between two people" (2009: 102). Yet I suggest that although the title of the song, 'Baby', suggests an intimate relationship, the lyrics are those of a generic love song. In contrast to so many of his pop songs, 'Baby' does not refer to a specific incident in Wainwright's life. To extend the analogy with Hall's scholarship, "a whisper has the effect of expanding the distance" (Hall, 1963: 1010).

The vocal on 'Poses', three years later, is in the close personal zone. The vocal sounds close to the listener, but it is a more rounded sound, a more complete vocal projection. Moore *et al.* explain that there is the possibility of intervening material, which can be heard here in the busy-ness of the track, which features a piano at the forefront, backing vocals, and a complete string section. Intake of breath can still be heard in 'Poses', but less clearly than in 'Baby'. Wainwright's use of the word "you" in the refrain "You said watch my head about it" could be addressed to one person, but the presence of a small group of backing singers makes it sound as though he is addressing a few people – again, adhering to Moore *et al.*'s suggestion of a small group. Lyrically, however, Wainwright has frequently alluded to the drug-ridden period of his life that 'Poses' refers to. As the content becomes more personal (to him), his style of vocal delivery moves along the spectrum to a more public style.

The opening of 'Old Whore's Diet', from *Want Two* (2004) features an even more rounded vocal style. It is at the forefront of the mix, with accompanying guitar far behind. However, the clarity of non-vocal sounds place this track towards the far side of the intimate zone (for example, the sharp intake of breath before the first vocals). As the song progresses, more layers of musical material (including Hegarty's guest vocal, backing vocals, and string section including ukelele and banjo) at times feature as prominently as the lead vocal line. The lyrical content refers to a specific moment in Rufus Wainwright's biography, in which he claims to have woken up from a drugs binge to find his fridge almost empty. But again, although "to say I love you" could refer to one person, it is ambiguous enough to mean any number of people.

'Do I Disappoint You', from 2007's *Release the Stars*, is in the social proxemic zone. Wainwright's vocal can be heard at a medium distance from the listener. There is little separation between the vocal persona and its musical environment, even though the voice sounds complete and medium-loud. As Moore *et al.* suggest for the social zone, there are few non-vocal sounds (an exception being the very quiet intake of breath at 1:52). Yet again, the lyrical content defies the table of criteria set up for vocal proxemics. The lyrics suggest a very intimate, personal subject matter, where Wainwright fears acceptance from his friends and family. The declamatory vocal style, on the other hand, suggests the opposite.

As an album, *All Days are Nights* does not fit the trend of the recorded vocal moving into the public proxemic zone while the subject material becomes more personal. The recorded vocal on 'Martha', for example, can be positioned in the far intimate proxemic zone. Wainwright's voice sounds close to the listener, and the piano accompaniment is positioned behind the voice. The vocal persona is set towards the front of the musical environment, but there is a good deal of interaction between the two elements. The addressing of the lyrical content to his sister Martha addresses the interpersonal relationship between the siblings, and textually refers to a specific period in their lives.

The title track from 2012's *Out of the Game* features a loud, declamatory vocal, and a high degree of intervening musical material (especially Thomas Brenneck's electric guitar). The vocals sound like an announcement, asserting the subject matter to all and sundry. The recording style is very clean, and no para-lingual sounds can be heard. These factors unite to place the track in the public zone of Moore *et al.*'s spatialization of recorded sound. Once again, however, the lyrical content does not match the proxemic categorization. One would expect the lyrics to be addressing a large group, whereas what we hear is an address to a single person: "Look at you ... You're only a child with the mind of a senile man ... Does your Mama know what you're doing? .... Let me smell you for one last time/Before you go out there and ruin all of the world once mine." The subject matter is personal, whereas the vocal style is public.

Over the course of all his studio albums, the proxemics, or spatialization, of the recorded vocal musically declares Wainwright's growing sense of self by transferring from the personal zone to the public. His willingness to share more and more private aspects of his autobiography while becoming more vocally declamatory illustrate the shift from the ego to the id explained with reference to sound-box analyses. His album dedications reflect this, as he transitions from a focus on his grandparents, to his fun-loving friends, to himself, and finally to the family members he wishes to care for.

Conclusion

Since I began this project in 2012, Rufus Wainwright has continued to be musically active. He has toured the *Out of the Game* material, with large-scale shows incorporating a full backing band and singers, and a surreal Dionysian encore. At the end of 2013, he featured on Robbie Williams's album of duets, *Swings Both Ways*. Rufus's contribution (after which the album is named) is a play on words, featuring a Sinatra-style swing feel, and lyrics passed between the two singers questioning each other's sexuality. In March 2014, he released *Vibrate: The Best of Rufus Wainwright*, which is comprised of reissues and new performances of his existing songs, with three new singles.[1] An associated tour of Europe and the USA (referred to as the "greatest hits" tour), took place in March and April 2014.

In March 2014, Wainwright announced a PledgeMusic campaign to crowd fund a recording of his opera *Prima Donna*, with the original cast members and the BBC symphony orchestra. Crowd funding is an increasingly popular phenomenon, which can be used to fund a wide variety of projects, including music, technology development, film literary works and software. Music is a particularly fertile area for crowd funding, as it helps to diminish the boundary between artist and fan. Artists or groups appeal to their fan base for the capital to produce their next work, requesting monetary advances on their forthcoming product, in exchange for which certain privileges are bestowed. Depending on the figure "pledged", or promised by the fan, artists often give insight into their creative process, or invite fans to participate in their public concerts, as well as a promised copy of their forthcoming work. Jazz composer Maria Schneider, for example, offered to conduct telephone calls with sponsors during the writing and rehearsal process of her albums *Concert in the Garden* (2005), *Sky Blue* (2007) and *Winter Morning Walks* (2013), all released through the company ArtistShare. Working with Kickstarter, popular singer-songwriter Amanda Palmer offers fans the opportunity to perform on stage with her in various tour venues, couching a search for local musicians as an exciting privilege for her fans. Companies such as Kickstarter, ArtistShare and PledgeMusic are representative of a development in the way artists interact with their fans in the digital age.[2] Artists gain an advance financial commitment from their fans, and in many cases an assured audience, because one of the cheaper offered rewards is often a copy of the promised album. The fan feels closer to the artist, because by "selling" insight into the artistic process, and details from their personal lives, the artist shares otherwise unseen information. Rufus Wainwright's adoption of this model to fund a recording of *Prima Donna* is fascinating, because he is wholeheartedly embracing an economic model more commonly associated with the popular music world, in order to finance his adventures into western art music.

Wainwright has chosen PledgeMusic as the vehicle to fund the *Prima Donna* recording. In his appeal, he offers a range of rewards, which fans can experience in the following four ways: insight into the creative process of *Prima Donna* (the opera); input into the production of *Prima Donna* (the recording), with no creative act on the part of the fan; general musical interaction with Rufus Wainwright; and items from Wainwright's personal life. In their forthcoming article on crowd funding, Williams and Wilson refer to items and experiences outside the musical product as "paratextual products". Financial pledges from fans have no upwards limit, but must be at least the prices suggested by PledgeMusic, which range from $15 to $60,000. Table 6.1 shows the options available. I have organized the paratextual products into four categories, and arranged rewards in order of suggested price. All products and paratextual products offered by Wainwright are of fixed availability: the limited edition creates feelings of exclusivity and desirability amongst pledgers. As Williams and Wilson note, this type of fan-artist interactivity plays a crucial role in the creation of online and offline identity of the artist (forthcoming 2016). Wainwright has a PledgeMusic website, which shows the amount of the financial goal reached. He and his management team frequently upload written, pictorial and video updates, of which a small amount can be seen by the general public, but the entire content is restricted to financial beneficiaries.

In addition to being able to secure a copy of the forthcoming recording, and being able to buy items from Wainwright's wardrobe and personal life, the rewards available allow differing degrees of artist fan interaction: from the straightforward transaction of buying an advance copy of a recording; to buying the right to take part in a "Hallelujah chorus", where Wainwright invites pledgers to join him onstage at various concert venues for a few bars of his cover of Leonard Cohen's hit; to various degrees of VIP treatment at concerts. The target sum was reached in June 2014. The site will remain open until the release of the recording, allowing pledgers to continue to access exclusive content, and fans to continue to buy items from the list. (The nature of the transaction implicitly changes at this point, for financial contributions are no longer strictly necessary to fund the recording.)[3]

In the winter of 2013, Wainwright announced that he had begun work on a large-scale grand opera based on the Roman Emperor Hadrian, with the working title *Hadrian*. After the chamber opera *Prima Donna*, *Hadrian* will be

Table 6.1: PledgeMusic rewards available for *Prima Donna* recording, March 2014

Type of Reward	Itemized Reward	Suggested Minimum Pledge
Prima Donna (the opera): creative/rehearsal process	Replicas of original *Prima Donna* costumes	$110
	Original piano-vocal rehearsal score	$450
	Conductor's baton from *Prima Donna* recording	$500
	Rufus's Opera Workshop score	$800
	Prima Donna full score, signed by Wainwright and the conductor	$1000
	Prima Donna messenger bag, from Manchester premiere	$300
Prima Donna (the recording): no creative input	*Prima Donna*: The album download and updates on recording process	$15
	Cast list signed by Rufus	$35
	Signed *Prima Donna* double CD	$40
	Double vinyl alum of *Prima Donna* recording	$65
	Your name in the liner notes (and a signed double CD)	$100
	Signed CD and signed vinyl	$100
	Vinyl test pressing, signed	$200
	Original album cover proof, signed	$750
	Impresario credit (executive producer credit in new album, and double signed CD)	$1000
	Prima Donna record producer credit and party	$1500
General musical interaction with Rufus Wainwright	Opportunity to join a Hallelujah chorus	$99
	Dedication of 'Les Feux d'Artifice' in concert	$250
	VIP concert experience (aftershow drink with Wainwright, opportunity to take photographs and attend sound check)	$750
	Signed full score of Shakespeare sonnets	$750
	Exclusive skype concert	$3000
	Private concert	$50,000
	Dinner and a song written about you	$60,000
Personal life/ celebrity paraphernalia	Original white wedding bracelets	$75
	Wedding programmes	$150
	Wedding portrait	$175
	Portraits of young Rufus	$150–175
	Outfits worn on tour and at publicity events	$150–5000
	Custom Rufus Wainwright shirts	$300
	Clogs worn by Rufus	$400
	Hello Kitty guitar played on 2012 *Out of the Game* tour	$2000
	Photo shoot with Wainwright (photographer = Tim Hailand)	$5000
Miscellaneous	One-hour singing lesson with Janis Kelly	$250

an expansion on an enormous scale. As Janis Kelly explained in 2013: "his next [opera] is going to be a huge piece ... thousands of people on stage, and huge choruses ... He doesn't feel the need to water anything down" (2013).

Hadrian is the first commission by the Canadian Opera Company (COC) for fifteen years, with a planned first performance on the mainstage session at the Four Seasons Centre in 2018.[4] Wainwright is collaborating with Canadian playwright Daniel MacIver, who will provide the libretto. Taken at surface value, Wainwright's second opera commission should represent an acceptance by the western art music establishment. However, his activities in the popular music sphere still affect his reception. Alexander Neef, COC's general director, has preemptively defended "the inevitable criticism he will face for having passed over more traditional Canadian composers to give a pop musician the COC's first commission in nearly 15 years". Neef says simply "It's a risk we have to take" (Harris, 2013). The debates between the art and popular music works that surround the commission of *Hadrian* show that tensions between the camps are far from over in public consciousness.

The schools of thought and systems of scholarship explained in this book are all limited in their own way: musicology from the western art music tradition is historically bound, be it Maynard Solomon and peers' early-1990s obsession with Schubert's sexuality, or the third-wave feminism of Catherine Clément and Carolyn Abbate. In comparison to the ripples in this long-established tradition, the discipline of popular music studies is relatively young and marginal, and the fight for academic legitimization was a subtext of many early entrants to the discourse and analysis. It is useful to think outside the binaries of classical/popular music and high/low art. In his 2011 book on jazz-rock fusion, Kevin Fellezs defines the grey area between traditionally opposed musics as the "broken middle". His summary of figures that bring together jazz and rock can be transposed exactly to illustrate Rufus Wainwright's fruitful union of techniques and traditions from western art music and popular music:

> [The] sounding out of the broken middle emphasizes individuals who do not fit neatly into given categories – or, more accurately, whose disheveled fit between categories allows them to challenge the displacement, misrecognition, and histories that seek to silence them. (2011: 228)

I close with two thoughts. First, I hope that my approach of blending methodologies associated with western art music and popular music helps give insight to fans, students and scholars from either field. This technique need not be restricted to the two idioms considered here; Fellezs's comments bring me full circle to my own scholarly starting point of classical music in jazz. Fellezs's exploration of jazz and rock fusions is another example of thinking outside expected generic norms in order to positively apply criteria and methodologies from a different field. I hope that readers of this book will think creatively about music of all idioms when applying analytical, discursive and evaluative criteria.

Rufus Wainwright's life and music have provided material aplenty for the methods used in this book: I have engaged with popular music formal analysis; queer theories and opera scholarship from the new musicology; music and geography; and sound-box and proxemic analysis of the virtual recorded space. As evidenced by the forthcoming *Hadrian*, and the PledgeMusic campaign to crowd fund a recording of *Prima Donna*, Rufus Wainwright continues to forge a career path within the popular and classical music traditions, in a manner that is uniquely his own. His life and music deserve more critical consideration, and I hope that the scholarly and fan communities rise to this challenge.

Notes

Introduction

1.   My description of Rufus Wainwright's live performance of 'Oh What a World' is an amalgamation of the performances featured at 36:00–38:00 on the documentary 2005 *All I Want*, and that on Alan Yentob's interview with Wainwright for the BBC documentary *Imagine* in July 2009.

2.   Richard Dyer (1986: 137–91) makes the connection between Garland and gay culture explicit in "Judy Garland and Gay Men", chapter 3 of *Heavenly Bodies: Film Stars and Society*. Wainwright extended his obsession with Judy Garland's portrayal of the central character by re-creating Garland's seminal 1961 Carnegie Hall concert in 2006, which I discuss further in Chapter 4.

Chapter 1

1.   Throughout this chapter, I distinguish between members of the Wainwright family by referring to them by their first names.

2.   Loudon Wainwright III autobiography, available at http://www.lw3.com/about. html (accessed 13 November 2012).

3.   Examples of folk styles and national colour also informed western art composers' works: for example Béla Bartók (Hungary 1881–1925) collected and utilized many folk styles in his instrumental music.

4.   The folk music revival is discussed more fully by Cantwell (1996), and Rosenburg (1993). Dave Laing *et al.* (1975) cover the transformation of acoustic folk into folk rock in the late 1960s.

5.   This movement is covered by Barker and Taylor (2007).

6.   I have provided a brief background to Loudon and Kate's musical background and meeting in order to explain the environment and musical tradition that Rufus was born into – a more detailed biography of Loudon and Kate is available in Lake (2009).

7.   Loudon appeared in three episodes of *M*A*S*H* in 1974–75. In 1979, he appeared in an unsuccessful pilot for a comedy *The T. V. Show* (featuring Rob Reiner, Christopher Guest and Harry Shearer). When comedian David Letterman originally hosted an afternoon talk show for NBC in 1980, Loudon was the original musical sideman – but he was dropped when the show moved to its well-known evening slot. For a short while in 1985, Loudon was the resident singer-songwriter for UK comedian Jasper Carrott's BBC show, but struggled to make satirical observations about a culture to which he did not belong. In 2000, Loudon played a small part in *28 Days*. Producer and screenwriter Judd Apatow had been impressed by the song 'Father and Son' on *History* (1992), and sought out Loudon to play the father in his dysfunctional family sit-com *Undeclared* (2001–2002). (The family was loosely based on the Wainwright model sketched out by Loudon in 'Father and Son'.) The Wainwright/Apatow collaboration extended further, with Apatow giving Loudon a

small role in 2005's *40-Year-Old Virgin*, and a larger role in 2007's *Knocked Up*. Loudon also contributed the soundtrack to *Knocked Up*, which he released as the album *Strange Weirdos*. In the intervening years, Loudon gained small roles in Tim Burton's 2003 *Big Fish*, Cameron Crowe's 2005 *Elizabethtown* and Martin Scorsese's *The Aviator* of the same year. He has also appeared in the TV shows *Ally McBeal* and *Parks and Recreation*.

8.   *Entre la Jeunesse et le Sagasse* (1981), *Love Over and Over* (1983), *Heartbeats Accelerating* (1990), *Matapédia* (1996) and *The McGarrigle Christmas Hour* (2005). Complete discographies for all Wainwright family members are provided in the bibliography.

9.   Wainwright comments: "Coming out to my parents was a nightmare. They reacted horrifically. There was fear, worry, shouting" (Shaitly, 2014).

10. Tony Whyton documents a parallel phenomenon surrounding famous jazz figures in "Witnessing and the Jazz Anecdote" (in 2010: 106–126).

11. Rufus has since made several film appearances and television appearances, including an appearance on the television series *Frasier* (2002), the films *The Aviator* (2004) and *Heights* (2005), a Christmas special of the BBC show *French and Saunders* (2005), the film *The Age of Ignorance* (2007), the television show *Dinner with the Band* (2010), *Rufus Does Gum* (film short, 2012) and the film *In the Woods* (2013). He has contributed songs and performances to numerous soundtracks including the films: *The Myth of Fingerprints* (1997), *Big Daddy* (1999), *Moulin Rouge* (2001), *Zoolander* (2001), *I am Sam* (2001), *Bridget Jones: The Edge of Reason* (2004), *The Aviator* (2004), *The Baxter* (2005), *Filthy Gorgeous: The Trannyshack Story* (2005), *Brokeback Mountain* (2005), *The History Boys* (2006), *Meet the Robinsons* (2007), *Quiet Chaos* (2008); television shows *Party of Five* (1999), *As Queer as Folk* (2002), *The O. C.* (2003), *Later with Jools Holland* (2004), *Druckfrisch* (2006), *Banda Sonora* (2008), *Dancing with the Stars* (2008), *So You Think You Can Dance* (2008–2009), *The New Paul O'Grady Show* (2009), *Die Harald Schmidt Series Show* (2012) and *De wereldt draait door* (2012); and television movies and documentaries *Leonard Cohen: I'm Your Man* (2005) and *Words to Music: The Canadian Songwriters Hall of Fame* (2006).

12. In 1995, the owner and organizers of Café Sarajevo moved the venue to the St Laurent area of the city, where it continues as a live music venue.

13. Roger Bourland, a Professor of Music Theory and Composition at the University of California Los Angeles, taught an entire undergraduate musicology module entitled "The Music of Rufus Wainwright" in spring 2006. The first session, entitled "family", included discussion of the three songs analysed in my evaluation of Rufus's relationships with Kate, Martha and Loudon. Bourland has posted brief notes about this class on his blog (available at www.rogerbourland.com, last accessed 14 January 2013), which indicate that this first session focused on lyrical analysis. I came to Bourland's writings after completing my own analyses.

14. Rufus and Loudon had recently featured in a *Rolling Stone* article about famous musical father-and-son pairings (Schruers, 1999: 61–94).

15. 'Romanticism' is the term used to cover the European arts in the first half of the nineteenth century. Musical features were: an expansion of the orchestra from the standard Classical instrumentation of strings, double woodwind and percussion; uneven phrase lengths; and chromatic and ambiguous harmony.

16. A history of the Royal Opera House is available at http://www.rohcollections.org.uk/ROHHistory.aspx (accessed 15 January 2013).

17. These messages are part of a strand entitled "Rufus and Loudon Wainwright III – ROH 21 July 2011", that developed in the days following the House of Rufus shows in late 2011. The entire discussion is available here: http://forums.rufuswainwright.com/index. php?/topic/52297-rufus-and-loudon-wainwright-iii-roh-21-july-2011/page__st__40 (accessed 15 January 2013).

18. Peggy Seeger is an American folksinger and activist who is herself the half-brother of folksinger Pete Seeger, and daughter of musician and musicologist Charles Seeger and composer and folk music specialist Ruth Crawford Seeger.

Chapter 2

1. I am not including *Vibrate*, his "best of" collection released in March 2014.

2. A roughly contemporaneous rock front man to use the piano is Ben Folds, who was active with the quirkily named quartet Ben Folds Five from 1995–2000. Folds focused on solo projects from 2000–2011, and the group reunited in 2011. Ben Folds and Rufus Wainwright performed George Michael's 'Careless Whisper' together on the Summer-stage of New York's Central Park on 13 July 2004. Wainwright thus places himself into the lineage of piano-playing popular music singer-songwriters (that includes Billy Joel, Elton John, Joni Mitchell, Tori Amos, Jamie Cullum and Jerry Lee Lewis). This tradition, though established, is in a minority to the guitar-playing norm.

3. I use the term "improvisatory" in reference to underlying large-scale melodic direction, with small-scale pitch and tempo alterations to the melody line. I discuss this phenomenon further in Williams (2012b). Wolfram Knaeur (1990) explains a similar concept in Duke Ellington's symphonic works.

4. Chambers is famous for co-writing many of the songs that helped launch Robbie Williams's solo career. He has written and produced for Kylie Minogue, Diana Ross, Beverley Knight, Andrea Boccelli, James Blunt, Tina Turner, Jamie Cullum, Katie Melua, Scissor Sisters, Tom Jones and The Wanted among others.

5. Warren has written for and with such diverse artists as Elton John, Cher, Barbra Streisand, Roy Orbison, Michael Bolton, N' Sync and Whitney Houston. Her songs have earned her six Academy Award nominations, five Golden Globe nominations including one win (2011, Best Original Song for 'You Haven't Seen the Last of Me' performed by Cher in the film *Burlesque*), and seven Grammy Award nominations including one win (1996, Best Song Written for a Motion Picture in *Up Close and Personal*).

6. "Lied" is the German singular, while "Lieder" is the plural. Wainwright is using the term incorrectly in this statement.

7. Nineteenth-century Viennese culture was forbidding towards homosexuality, and repressive in its intolerance. Schubert's activities would therefore have been conducted within an environment of outsiders, providing grounding for the isolation and oppression associated with his music. When Maynard Solomon "outed" Schubert in the late 1980s, it provoked a famous musicological debate. Solomon's 1989 article in *19th-Century Music* prompted heated discourse amongst respected scholars in the following years. Solomon's revelation that Schubert may have been homosexual was greeted with abject horror, and rebutted by fellow academics such as Rita Steblin (1992, 1993). An entire issue of the journal *19th-Century Music* was devoted to the controversy in 1993, edited by Lawrence Kramer. This episode betrays an expected heteronormativity in western art music

and study of the tradition at the time – an expectation that is supported by the relatively few openly homosexual composers and those that (like Schubert and Tchaikovsky) kept their personal lives private. Schwandt suggests that Wainwright knowingly connects with these expectations and debates: "There is every reason to believe that the 'erudite' and self-affirmed 'Classical' snob Wainwright is aware, and probably titillated by this scholarly episode" (2010: 161 n. 168).

8.   Unusual composer spellings are reproduced as in the Yellow Lounge listing. Commonly accepted spellings are "Shostakovich", "Tchaikovsky".

9.   Petronio had extended *Bud* to included four Wainwright songs ('Oh What a World', 'Vibrate', 'This Love Affair' and 'Agnus Dei'). *Bud Suite* was a backup in case Wainwright had not completed the score for *BLOOM*, and in the event, the former was used as an opener for the latter (Lake, 2009: 15). Petronio became the Joyce Theatre's first Artist-in-Residence in the 2012–13 season.

10.   The sonnets set to music were: 43, 148, 76, 53, 18, 10, 121, 91, 20, 40, 143, 102, 29, 23, 144, 127, 147, 66, 113, 107, 71, 44, 129, 87, 154.

11.   A type of vocal delivery midway between speech and song.

12.   Kelly recalled reading about Wainwright's forthcoming project in a magazine a year or two earlier. She was already familiar with the music of the Wainwright family, and claims to have been very affected by Rufus's desire to write an opera. She looked up the location of his next performance, and sent him a letter of support, offering her help in practical ways, "never for a moment dreaming that I'd be in it". The letter never reached Wainwright, but they have since laughed about her "message into the ether" (Kelly, 2013). This anecdote is also reported in Harries (2010).

13.   Exceptions are track 4, which was co-produced by Rufus Wainwright and Pierre Marchand, and tracks 10 and 11, which were entirely produced by Marchand.

14.   Decca was founded as a British label in 1929, with a US branch following in 1934. The link between the two companies was broken for a long time during the war, but eventually both companies were subsumed into the Universal Music Group. More information is available at the Decca website: www.decca.com (accessed 29 October 2013).

15.   I am grateful to my husband Justin Williams for this initial observation.

16.   Amos helped Wainwright emotionally, when he joined her on her StrangeLittleTour at the end of 2001. In her song 'Me and a Gun', Amos revisited being raped after a concert at the age of twenty-one. Through the song, and the Rape, Abuse and Incest National Network charity for which she was its early spokesperson, she helped Wainwright revisit and move on from a sexual assault he suffered in London's Hyde Park at the age of fourteen.

17.   Further similarities can be noted between Wainwright and Amos. Both Wainwright's *Out of the Game* (2012) and Amos's *Unrepentant Geraldines* (2014) were heralded as a long-awaited return to pop after more classically influenced material.

Chapter 3

1.   Aristotle Onassis had left Maria Callas for Jackie (whom he later married) in 1968, and by playing Callas's records in Mrs Onassis's hometown, Wainwright hoped to show that he felt Callas had been mistreated. This perception overlooks the fact that Callas's relationship with the Greek shipping magnate had begun when they were both married to other people (Jellinek, 1960: 270–92).

2. Clément's book was published during a transitional time in musicological study, when the existing norm of positivistic and analytical approaches was challenged by the socially situated new musicology of such scholars as Susan McClary, Gary Tomlinson, Lawrence Kramer, Jeffrey Kallberg, Richard Taruskin and Philip Bohlman. The new influences they brought to musicology included feminism, queer theory, gender studies, post-colonial studies, structuralism and post-structuralism. Value judgements were no longer based solely upon thematic unity and organicism – indeed, new musicologists frequently attacked these criteria. In 1995 musicologist Carolyn Abbate responded to Clément with "Opera, or the Envoicing of Women", in which she concurred that operatic heroines were killed on stage every night by their male creators – but argued that the beautiful, virtuosic and challenging music assigned to these women in their dying moments actually amounted to their *empowerment*. Historically, Abbate argues, opera has had the capacity to disrupt male authority. "Opera, with *music* that subverts the borders we fix between the sexes, speaks for the envoicing of women" (in Solie, ed., 1995: 258).

3. Metzer (2003) applies and explains this methodology in a range of case studies, including: nostalgia in the works of Charles Ives; Ellington's use of spirituals in *Black and Tan Fantasy*; madness evoked by thematic recall in opera; reworking of compositions in the works of Berio, Rochberg and Oswald; sampling; and cover versions.

4. The plot of *Carmen* can be briefly summarized thus: The opera opens with a view onto a tobacco factory backing onto a guardroom in Seville. The male protagonist Don José's sweet and girlish fiancé Micaëla enters, looking for him. His soldier compatriots inform her that he is not yet back at the guardroom. She declines their offer to wait with them, and leaves. Don José arrives shortly after. The crowd in the square watch the cigarette girls go by as they return from their lunch break. Carmen (a cigarette worker herself) arrives with a flower in her mouth, followed by a bevy of admirers. She sings her famous habanera 'L'amour est une oiseau rebelle', explaining that she believes "love is something to be seized when it passes" (Macdonald, n.d.). Her aria includes the line "If I love you, take care!", issuing a warning for the future. Don José falls in love with Carmen the seductress over the dutiful Micaëla. A fight between Carmen and another girl breaks out in the factory. Don José helps Carmen escape from the situation, and is sent to prison for his role in the fight.

On his release, Don Jose fights with the toreador Escamillo over Carmen's virtue. Escamillo invites Don José to attend his next bullfight in Seville (Bizet's bullfighting song, "Toreador", is also famous). At the bullfight, Carmen denies loving Don José and calls their relationship off. Don José stabs her in the heat of passion, while Escamillo is triumphant in the bullfight. Carmen contains all the elements of a successful opera: love, death and drama. For a more detailed plot summary, see Macdonald (n.d.).

5. Smith continues to explain his thesis of Wainwright-as-opera-queen, citing two reworkings of the Orpheus myth in Wainwright's output. Through close readings of 'Memphis Skyline' and 'Waiting for a Dream' (amongst more superficial readings of other songs), he explains Wainwright's use of the common operatic plot. These devices, he suggests, support his perception of Wainwright as an opera queen. Kevin C. Schwandt makes a similar argument in the chapter 'For My Harp I Have Strung': Orpheus and Queer Authority" (2010: 73–99).

Chapter 4

1.   Sara Cohen in her chapter on music scenes (Horner and Swiss, eds. 1999), and *Decline, Renewal and the City in Popular Music Culture: Beyond the Beatles* (2007); Daniel Grimley in *Grieg: Music, Landscape and Norwegian Identity* (2007) and Adam Krims's *Music and Urban Geography* (2007). *Music, Space and Place*, edited by Sheila Whiteley, Andy Bennett and Stan Hawkins, brings together a thoughtful collection of essays that interrogate space and nationhood in music, place in rap, and the gendered possibilities of virtual space in production (2004). In his article "'Represent': Race, Space and Place in Rap Music" (2000), and his subsequent monograph *The 'Hood Comes First: Race, Space and Place in Rap and Hip-Hop* (2002), Murray Forman examines the crucial role of the local neighbourhood in the construction of gang pride and sonic identity in rap music. In nuanced and insightful analyses, he juxtaposes the locally identified beginnings with potential loss of identity as a hip-hop artist's star rises in an increasingly decentralized record marketplace, and the construction and commercial reinforcement of a physical and ideological "hip-hop nation" divided by geographical (coastal) lines.

2.   After hearing Buckley's version of Leonard Cohen's 'Hallelujah' (released on Buckley's only complete studio album, *Grace*, 1994), Wainwright wrote 'Memphis Skyline' as a tribute to the singer (featured on *Want Two*). Kevin C. Schwandt offers a fascinating interpretation of 'Memphis Skyline' and the following song on *Want One*, 'Waiting for a Dream'. He suggests that taken together, these songs form a contemporary, queer reinterpretation of the Orpheus myth (2010: 91–99).

3.   Wainwright was among the first musicians to be signed to DreamWorks. Others included George Michael and alternative rock bands Morphine and Eels.

4.   The importance of the Chelsea Hotel to popular music history is documented and mythologized by Joe Ambrose. In *Chelsea Hotel Manhattan* (2007), through prose, collected journalism and transcripts of interviews, he describes exploits and meetings with Andy Warhol, the New York Dolls, Debbie Harry and Patti Smith among others.

5.   This movement was focused around trends in American rhythm and blues, but geographically centred in UK dance halls and nightclubs such as the Twisted Wheel in Manchester, the Blackpool Mecca and Wigan Casino. The heavy syncopated beats and fast tempi of mid-1960s Motown, combined with soulful vocals (for example Gladys Knight's 1964 'Tainted Love') bore no resemblance to indigenous musical trends of northern Britain, but became associated with the region in cultural memory.

6.   See Cohen (2007: 32–33) for a more detailed description of the Merseybeat sound.

7.   Glass funded the Philip Glass Ensemble himself for eleven years by taking on odd jobs; working at times as a plumber, a taxi driver and a crane operator to supplement his musical income and retain his ensemble with a steady salary (Potter, 2000: 260). Despite Glass's prolific output as a youthful composer (by the end of his period in Pittsburgh, he had composed over seventy works, many of which were published), his breakthrough came in 1975, when he collaborated with theatre director Robert Wilson on *Einstein on the Beach*. The Philip Glass Ensemble's early performances were a combination of informal performances in Glass's Bleeker Street loft apartment, and formal concerts in downtown Manhattan art galleries (Duckworth, 1995: 319).

8.   'The Art Teacher' is one of the few Rufus Wainwright songs published as sheet music. The music examples here are taken from the official 'Put Tit On' publication, and any harmonic ambiguity should be taken as intended by the composer.

9. Two examples from the vast range of possibilities in the classical canon are the bells of Big Ben heard in Ralph Vaughan Williams's Symphony No. 2 ('A London Symphony') and the sweeping pastoral landscapes evoked by Edvard Grieg's output (as suggested by Grimley, 2007).

10. A member of Rufus Wainwright's fan message board, who is paraphrasing the now unavailable online commentaries to *Want Two*, makes this observation. Available at: http://forums.rufuswainwright.com/index.php?/topic/44333-14th-street-discussion-of-track-8/page__st__160 (accessed 4 April 2014).

11. This list of Wainwright studio songs containing lyrical references to specific places is representative rather than exhaustive. A more extensive list follows: 'Foolish Love', 'Danny Boy', 'Millbrook', 'Barcelona' (*Rufus Wainwright*); 'Poses', 'California', 'The Tower of Learning' (*Poses*); 'I Don't Know What It Is', '14th Street', '11.11' (*Want One*); 'The One You Love', 'Peach Trees', 'Hometown Waltz', 'Memphis Skyline', 'Waiting for a Dream' (*Want Two*); 'Tiergarten', 'Between My Legs', 'Sanssoucci', 'Release the Stars' (*Release the Stars*); 'Jericho' (*Out of the Game*).

12. Full instrumentation and vocals of 'California' are as follows: Rufus Wainwright: acoustic guitar, piano, dobro, vocals; Jeff Hill: bass, backing vocals; Richard Causon: Chamberlin, Wurlitzer, Hammond B3, backing vocals; Butch: drums and percussion; Ethan Johns: electric guitars; Julianna Raye, Teddy Thompson and Martha Wainwright: backing vocals.

13. Lake expands further on Wainwright's reasons for writing 'California', which he performed live in between the release of his first and second albums. "'California' [was] a garage-pop song which was Rufus' response to too long spent in Los Angeles while recording his debut … 'The song itself is kind of tongue in cheek … I'd been living in LA making my first record, and working with Van Dyke Parks and Jon Brion. All my players were West Coast and there was this kind of Beach Boys sound we were going for. It occurred to me that I was a West Coast artist all of a sudden and that was a kind of nightmarish experience … I was becoming very California and I wrote that song to make me aware of that'" (Wainwright in Lake, 2009: 146–47). The "Beach Boys sound" Wainwright refers to can be expanded to include 1960s folk-rock figures and groups such as The Byrds, Neil Young, and Crosby, Stills and Nash.

14. These descriptors are set out in "A Hermeneutics of Recorded Song" (Moore, Schmidt and Dockwray, 2009: 103–104).

15. A helpful comparison can be drawn with Christopher Small's observation that audiences entering art music venues observe concert etiquette as though they were following a religious ritual (1998: 23).

16. In anatomical terms, he is tilting his crichoid (ring of cartilage surrounding the vocal chords) in order to further project his voice. I am grateful to Sonum Batra for her advice in this analysis of Wainwright's singing style.

17. I was also in attendance at this performance, and draw the following analysis from my own recollections as well as filmed recordings available online.

18. For example, his Spring-Summer 2014 US-Europe tour incorporates the following art music venues and large-scale festivals: Kucukciftlik Park, Istanbul, Turkey (11/4/2014); Town Hall, New York (15/4/14); Lincoln Theatre, Washington DC (16/4/14); Orpheum Theatre, Los Angeles, CA (18/4/14); Palace of Fine Arts, San Francisco, CA (19-20/4/14); Le Cargo, Caen, France (23/4/14); Le Printemps de Bourges, Bourges, France (24/4/14);

La Gaîté lyrique, Paris, France (25/4/14); Warwick Arts Centre, Coventry, UK (27/4/14); Luminato Presents If I Loved You: Gentlemen Prefer Broadway – An Evening of Love Duets – Song Centre For the Performing Arts, Toronto, ON, Canada (14/6/14); Somerville Theater, Somerville, MA (18/6/14); Westhampton Beach Performing Arts Center, Westhampton, NY (20/6/14); Clearwater Festival, Croton on Hudson, NY (21/6/14); The Kent Stage, Kent, OH (22/6/14); Weesner Family Amphitheater, Apple Valley, MN (24/6/14); Pavinia Festival, Highland Park, IL (25/6/14); Théâtre du Nouveau Monde, Montréal, Canada (27-29/6/14); Longwood Gardens, Open Air Theatre, Kennett Square, PA (1/7/14); Auditorium Parco della Musica, Rome, Italy (3/7/14); Days Off Festival, La Salla Pleyel, Paris, France (6/7/14); Pappy + Harriet's Pioneertown Palace, Pioneertown, CA (17/7/14); Aspen Music Festival, Aspen, CO (24/7/14).

19. Garland's set list ran: Overture/'The Trolley Song'/'Over The Rainbow'/'The Man That Got Away'; 'When You're Smiling (The Whole World Smiles With Me)'; Medley: 'Almost Like Being in Love'/'This Can't Be Love'; 'Do It Again', 'You Go To My Head'; 'Alone Together'; 'Who Cares? (As Long As You Care For Me)'; 'Puttin' On The Ritz'; 'How Long Has This Been Going On'; 'Just You, Just Me'; 'The Man that Got Away'; 'San Francisco'; 'That's Entertainment'; 'I Can't Give You Anything But Love'; 'Come Rain or Come Shine'; 'You're Nearer'; 'A Foggy Day'; 'If Love Were All'; 'Zing! Went the Strings of My Heart'; 'Stormy Weather'; Medley: 'You Made Me Love You'/'For Me and My Gal'/'The Trolley Song'; 'Rock-A-Bye Your Baby With a Dixie Melody'; 'Over The Rainbow'; 'Swanee'; 'After You've Gone'; 'Chicago'. In Rufus Wainwright's version of the concert, Martha sang 'Stormy Weather', Kate featured on the vocal version of 'Over the Rainbow', and Lorna Luft featured on 'After You've Gone'. Encores were 'Get Happy'; 'Hello Bluebird' (starring Lorna Luft); 'Someone to Watch Over Me' (starring Martha and Kate); 'Everytime We Say Goodbye' (featuring Kate) and a reprise of 'San Francisco'.

20. Wainwright's song '14th Street' (*Want One*) contains the line "they'll be rainbows", which is a reference to a line from 'Over the Rainbow'. 'Over the Rainbow' was an important part of Garland's career, featuring in *The Wizard of Oz*, and forming part of her repertoire thereafter.

21. Carnegie Hall is a culturally significant venue in and of itself: since it was opened as a dedicated classical-music performance space in 1891 with a performance conducted by Pyotr Ilyich Tchaikovsky, it has become a marker for acceptance within the western art music world. In the mid-1900s, several "jazz concerts" took place in Carnegie Hall, elevating jazz from a music heard on the street and in dance halls to a concert-worthy art form (Williams, 2012a). By performing in Carnegie Hall, Wainwright not only recreates the seminal Garland concert, but appropriates some of the cultural prestige of the venue.

Chapter 5

1. Moore and Dockwray's initial investigation considers rock music from 1965–72, and their analyses are based around the utilization of what they understand to be the three key elements of this period: lead guitar, bass guitar and snare drum. My analyses use different key elements, because Wainwright frequently writes for piano and voice, rather than the guitar-based compositions that form the core of Moore *et al.*'s work. Dockwray and Moore base their sound-boxes on a cumulative analysis of the entire tracks in question (Dockwray and Moore, 2008, 2010; Moore, 2010). I have adapted their methodology

for the purposes of this study: I refer to 20–40 second "snapshot" transcriptions, focusing on specific, clearly identified extracts of songs. Each chosen song is a well-known and commercially successful representation of the musical style of the album in question, and offers insight into Wainwright's biography.

2. Dockwray and Moore's study involved the transcription of 1000 tracks from the UK and US charts in the years 1966–72. Using both loudspeaker and headphone analysis, they plotted the sounds onto the sound-box. Rather than creating several different transcriptions for a song whose sonic image changes throughout the duration, the final sound-box analyses are a cumulative visual representation (Dockwray and Moore, 2010: 183–85).

This framework is dependent on the human ear and perception for two stages of the perceptual process: both for determining the sonic positioning of instruments, and for suggesting a visual representation indicative of the entire track. The subjectivity of this working method could be viewed as a weakness, for each individual listener hears songs in a different way. However, as Moore asserts in his 2012 book *Song Means*, songs create a specific meaning for each listener, based on the listener's prior knowledge of experiencing and making music. Following Moore's compelling argument, I propose that if the creation of meaning of recorded popular song can be subjective, so too should its analysis. My methodology differs slightly from that of Dockwray and Moore. I analyse each track in question by listening through in-built laptop speakers (a MacBook Air, to be precise), and again through AKG MkII open-ear and Sennheiser HD 485 closed-ear headphones. I believe that these listening methods are representative of standard playback methods of the early 2000s and 2010s, which gives me an understanding of the ways in which Rufus Wainwright's recorded output is usually heard. Rather than the complete track, I refer to 20–40 second extracts of tracks, which are clearly identified, and contain one sound world throughout.

3. Kirk Lake states that 'Danny Boy' is the second of a pair of love songs to Danny, with the first, 'Foolish Love', marking the beginning of the infatuation, and 'Danny Boy' the end (2009: 72).

4. My thanks to Joe Bennett, who offered helpful suggestions from the perspective of a producer upon delivery of this chapter in paper form at July 2013's popMAC conference in Liverpool. He suggested quantifying the elements of the mix, and analysing the different components statistically. Unfortunately it is impossible to separate out the components of an already mixed recording. Such analysis has fruitfully been carried out by Timothy Hughes, in his PhD dissertation on the music of Stevie Wonder. Hughes was able to break down the recordings to "stems" of the music, and analyse exactly how prominent each stem (or small cell) was in recorded songs (Hughes, 2003: 107–139).

5. I analyse only one example from the *Want* sessions. Although they were released as two albums, they were composed and recorded at the same time, and can be considered part of the same era of musical development.

6. Sigmund Freud provided a definitive theory of his psychoanalysis in his 1923 text *The Ego and the Id*. The "super-ego", he explained, is the moralizing and critical part of the mind. He categorized the "ego" as the conscious, coherent organization of mental processes. Any processes that are manifested externally, he writes, belong to the ego (Freud, 1923, reprinted in Gay, ed., 1995: 630). The "id", Freud explains, is the entirety of an individual's self, which is unknown and unconscious, and yet represents deep-seated desires

and passions. The ego rests upon the id. Freud writes: "The ego is not sharply separated from the id; its lower portion merges into it" (*ibid.*: 635).

7.   The official UK release of *Want Two* contained two live tracks, both are which are in French. Tracks 13 ('Couer de Parisienne—Reprise d'Arletty') and 14 ('Quand vous mourez de nos amours') feature Rufus accompanying himself on piano, and the latter also features soft backing vocals from Kate and Anna McGarrigle.

8.   *Release the Stars* personnel: Rufus Wainwright (vocals, piano, orchestral arrangement); Larry Mullins (shaker, triangle, glockenspiel, cymbals, cowbells, timpani, bells, bass drum, tambourine, vibes, piano percussion); Martha Wainwright (backing vocals); Neil Tennant (samples, loops); Rahel Rilling (violin); Gabriel Adorján (violin); Raphael Sacks (viola); Dávid Adorján (cello); Jeff Hill (bass); Ozan Cakar (French horn); Florian Dörpholz (trumpet); Raphael Mentzen (trumpet); Pirmin Grehl (flute); Gerry Leonard (guitar); Steven Bernstein (conductor, lead trumpet); Dave Trigg (trumpet, piccolo trumpet); John Chudoba (trumpet); Dominic Derasse (trumpet, piccolo trumpet); Carl Albach (trumpet, piccolo trumpet); Dan Levine (trombone); Marius de Vries and Jason Boshoff (programming).

9.   It is difficult to untangle the percussive harmony instrument heard in the middle background of the mix from the complete blended accompaniment sound. It is listed in the CD credits as "piano percussion", and sounds to me as though the strings inside the piano were being struck with a mallet. This would be inconvenient to play with clarity in live performance as the strings are very close together. My suspicion is that the sounds have been recorded in isolation, and then recreated at a higher speed through a sampler, but this is guesswork.

10.   Except for track 4, which was co-produced by Rufus Wainwright and Pierre Marchand, and tracks 10 and 11, which were entirely produced by Marchand.

11.   The liner notes to *All Days are Nights* are handwritten in a characterful, loopy handwriting, credited to Jörn Weisbrodt. The tails and crosses of the letters are particularly flamboyant. Graphology, or the study of handwriting, suggests a person that writes like this, with the letter tails extending far beneath the letters, is focused on history. Rufus Wainwright's autobiographical songs reinforce this view.

12.   Lineages and legacies abound in this name. "Viva" is an Italian term, often used in music to mean "lively", or in social discourse to mean "long live". "Katherine" continues Kate's heritage, while "Wainwright Cohen" spell out the line of singer-songwriters that have led to this child.

Conclusion

1.   'WWIII' is the song he co-wrote with Guy Chambers for the 2011 BBC documentary *Secrets of the Pop Song*, and 'Chic and Pointless' and 'Me & Liza' were released as singles.

2.   A table with a comprehensive comparison of the existing music crowd funding companies is available in Williams and Wilson (forthcoming 2016).

3.   The release date was initially set as April 2015. After a short delay, digital downloads of the opera were released on 11 September 2015, and physical copies on 5 October of the same year.

4.   Since 1999, two further commissions were made by the COC, but neither reached performance.

Bibliography

Abbate, Carolyn. 1995. "Opera: Or, the Envoicing of Women." In *Musicology and Difference: Gender and Sexuality in Music Scholarship*, ed. Ruth A. Solie, 225–58. Berkeley and Los Angeles: University of California Press.

Abel, Sam. 1996. *Opera in the Flesh: Sexuality in Operatic Performance*. Boulder, CO: Westview Press.

Adams, Tim. 2005. "Crystal Clear." *Observer Music Monthly*, 20 February.

Ambrose, Joe. 2007. *Chelsea Hotel Manhattan*. London: Headpress.

Amos, Tori. 2011. "Tori Amos Makes her Deutsche Grammophon Debut with 'Night of Hunters'." 5 May. http://www.deutschegrammophon.com/en/gpp/index/tori-amos-debut (accessed 2 December 2013).

Anonymous. Billboard 200. http://www.billboard.com/artist/369279/rufus-wainwright/chart (accessed 17 January 2014).

Anonymous. Rufus Wainwright message boards. http://forums.rufuswainwright.com/index.php?/topic/41412-shakespeare-sonnets-berlin-april-2009/page__st__280 (accessed 17 February 2014).

Barber, Simon and Brian O'Connor. 2014. *Sodajerker on Songwriting featuring Rufus Wainwright*. 26 February. 55 minutes. Available through iTunes podcast.

Barker, Hugh and Yuval Taylor. 2007. *Faking it: The Quest for Authenticity in Popular Music*. New York and London: W. W. Norton & Company.

Barthes, Roland. 1977. "The Grain of the Voice." In *Image Music Text*, 179–89. London: Fontana Press.

Barulich, Frances, and Jan Fairley. n.d. "Habanera." *Oxford Music Online*. http://www.oxfordmusiconline.com/subscriber/article/grove/music/12116?q=habanera&search=quick&pos=1&_start=1#firsthit (accessed 4 June 2013).

Behrend, Eva. 2009. "Rufus Wainwright über die Inszenierung der Shakespeare-Sonnette." *Tip Berlin*, Ausgabe 8. http://www.tip-berlin.de/kultur-und-freizeit-theater-und-buehne/rufus-wainwright-uber-die-inszenierung-der-shakespeare-sonett#car (accessed 17 February 2014).

Bennett, Andy, Barry Shank and Jason Toynbee. 2006. "Introduction." In *The Popular Music Studies Reader*, ed. Bennett, Shank and Toynbee, 1–10. London and New York: Routledge.

Bennett, Joe. 2013. "'You Won't See Me': In Search of an Epistemology of Collaborative Songwriting." *Journal on the Art of Record Production* (December). http://arpjournal.com/"you-won't-see-me"---in-search-of-an-epistemology-of-collaborative-songwriting/ (accessed 29 October 2015).

Bourland, Roger. 2006. "UCLA Seminar: The Music of Rufus Wainwright #6." 28 February.

http://rogerbourland.com/2006/02/28/ucla-seminar-the-music-of-rufus-wainwright-6/ (accessed 24 March 2014).

Cantwell, Robert. 1996. *When We Were Good: The Folk Revival.* Cambridge, MA: Harvard University Press.

Cenciarelli, Carlo. 2013. "At the Margins of the Televisual: Picture Frames, Loops, and 'Cinematics' in the Paratexts of Opera Videos." *Cambridge Opera Journal* 25, no. 2: 203–223.

Charlton, David, ed. 2003. *The Cambridge Companion to Grand Opera.* Cambridge: Cambridge University Press.

Christgau, Robert. 1998. "Rufus Wainwright: *Rufus Wainwright.*" *Spin*, July. http://www.robertchristgau.com/xg/cdrev/rufus-spi.php (accessed 2 July 2015).

Clément, Catherine. 1988. *Opera, or the Undoing of Women.* Minneapolis and London: University of Minnesota Press. First published in France 1979, English translation by Betsy Wing.

Clements, Andrew. 2010. "Prima Donna." *The Guardian*, 13 April. http://www.theguardian.com/music/2010/apr/13/prima-donna-review (accessed 21 July 2015).

Cohen, Norm. n.d. "Folk Music." Grove Music Online. *Oxford Music Online.* Oxford University Press. http://www.oxfordmusiconline.com/subscriber/article/grove/music/A2241135 (accessed 24 July 2015).

Cohen, Sara. 1999. "Scenes." In *Key Terms in Popular Music and Culture*, ed. Bruce Horner and Thomas Swiss, 239–50. Oxford: Blackwell.

—2007. *Decline, Renewal and the City in Popular Music Culture: Beyond the Beatles.* Aldershot: Ashgate.

Covach, John, and Andrew Flory. 2012. *What's That Sound? An Introduction to Rock and its History*, 3rd edn. New York and London: W. W. Norton & Company. First published 2006.

Dahlhaus, Carl. 1989. *Nineteenth-Century Music.* Berkeley and Los Angeles: University of California Press. First published in Germany, 1980. English translation by J. Bradford Robinson.

Davis, Sheila. 1985. *The Craft of Lyric Writing.* London/New York/Sydney: Omnibus Press.

Dockwray, Ruth, and Allan F. Moore. 2008. "The Establishment of the Virtual Performance Space in Rock." *Twentieth-century Music* 5, no. 2: 218–41.

—2010. "Configuring the Sound-box 1965–72." *Popular Music* 29, no. 2: 181–97.

Duckworth, William. 1995. *Talking Music: Conversations with John Cage, Philip Glass, Laurie Anderson, and Five Generations of American Experimental Composers.* New York: Schirmer Books.

Dunning, Jennifer. 2006. "Rufus Wainwright as Muse: Stephen Petronio's 'Bud Suite' and 'Bloom' at the Joyce." *New York Times*, 20 April. http://www.nytimes.com/2006/04/20/arts/dance/20petr.html (accessed 31 January 2014).

Dyer, Richard. 1986. *Heavenly Bodies: Film Stars and Society.* London and New York: Routledge.

Everett-Green, Robert. 2010. "The Best and Worst of Times for Rufus Wainwright." *The Globe and Mail*, 19 March. https://web.archive.org/web/20100323055710/http://www.theglobeandmail.com/news/arts/the-best-and-worst-of-times-for-rufus-wainwright/article1506000/ (accessed 23 June 2014).

Fairley, Jan, and Frances Barulich. n.d. "Habanera." *Grove Music Online/Oxford Music Online*. http://www.oxfordmusiconline.com/subscriber/article/grove/music/12116 (accessed 24 June 2014).

Fellezs, Kevin. 2011. *Birds of Fire: Jazz, Rock, Funk, and the Creation of Fusion*. Durham, NC and London: Duke University Press.

Forman, Murray. 2000. "'Represent': Race, Space and Place in Rap Music." *Popular Music* 19, no. 1: 65–90.

—2002. *The 'Hood Comes First: Race, Space and Place in Rap and Hip-Hop*. Middletown, CT: Wesleyan University Press.

Freud, Sigmund. 1995. *The Ego and the Id*. In *The Freud Reader*, ed. Peter Gay, 628–58. New York and London: W. W. Norton & Company. First published in German, 1923.

Gay, Peter, ed. 1995. *The Freud Reader*. New York and London: W. W. Norton & Company.

Gergen, Kenneth J. 1991. *The Saturated Self: Dilemmas of Identity in Contemporary Life*. New York: Basic Books.

Gibbs, Christopher H. 1997. "Introduction: The Elusive Schubert." In *The Cambridge Companion to Schubert*, ed. Gibbs, 1–14. Cambridge: Cambridge University Press.

Gibbs, Christopher H., ed. 1997. *The Cambridge Companion to Schubert*. Cambridge: Cambridge University Press.

Giltz, Michael. 2001. "The World According to Rufus." *The Advocate*, 8 May: 38–39.

Graff, Gary. 2001. "Rufus Wainwright: I'm Totally Selling Out." *ABC News*, 9 May. http://abcnews.go.com/Entertainment/story?id=105416 (accessed 2 July 2015).

Grimley, Daniel M. 2007. *Grieg: Music, Landscape and Norwegian Identity*. Woodbridge: Boydell Press.

Grover-Friedlander, Michael. 2006. "The Afterlife of Maria Callas's Voice." *The Musical Quarterly* 88, no. 1: 35–62.

Haight, Lisa. 2006. "Stephen Petronio Company in Lareigne/Bud Suite/Bloom at Queen Elizabeth Hall." *London Dance*, 25 October. http://londondance.com/articles/reviews/lareigne-bud-suite-bloom-at-queen-elizabeth--419/ (accessed 21 July 2015).

Hall, Edward T. 1963. "A System for the Notation of Proxemic Behavior." *American Anthropologist* 65, no. 3: 1003–1026.

—1966. *The Hidden Dimension*. London: Bodley Head.

—1969. "Proxemics." *Current Anthropology* 9, nos 2–3: 83–108.

Harries, Rhiannon. 2010. "How We Met: Janis Kelly and Rufus Wainwright." *The Independent on Sunday*, 21 March. http://www.independent.co.uk/news/people/profiles/how-we-met-janis-kelly--rufus-wainwright-1922854.html (accessed 6 December 2013).

Harris, Robert. 2013. "Why Rufus Wainwright is Turning a Roman Emperor into a COC Opera." *The Globe and Mail*, 30 November. http://www.theglobeandmail.com/arts/theatre-and-performance/how-rufus-wainwright-is-turning-a-roman-emperor-into-a-coc-opera/article15677143/?page=2 (accessed 2 December 2013).

Hattenstone, Simon. 2007. Interview with Rufus Wainwright. "Verdi and Me." *The Guardian*, 14 April. http://guardian.co.uk/music/2007/apr/14/popandrock.features/print (accessed 7 September 2012).

Higgins, Charlotte. 2008. "From Pop to Opera: Petrified Rufus Wainwright Embraces 'the Dark Religion'." *The Guardian*, 9 October. http://www.guardian.co.uk/music/2008/oct/09/rufuswainwright.folk#ixzz2UgsSDM00 (accessed 29 May 2013).

Horner, Bruce, and Thomas Swiss, eds. 1999. *Key Terms in Popular Music and Culture*. Oxford: Blackwell.

Hossbach, Martin. 2007. Liner notes to *Yellow Lounge compiled by Rufus Wainwright*. Deutsche Grammophon/Universal Music Classics & Jazz. 00289 442 9153. Translated by Janet and Michael Berridge.

Hughes, Timothy S. 2003. "Groove and Flow: Six Analytical Essays on the Music of Stevie Wonder." PhD dissertation, University of Washington.

Jellinek, George. 1960. *Callas: Portrait of a Prima Donna*. Reprinted 1986. New York: Dover.

Jones, Matthew J. 2002. "All These Poses, Such Beautiful Poses: Articulations of Queer Masculinity in the Music of Rufus Wainwright." MA thesis, University of Georgia.

Kelly, Janis. 2013. Interview with the Author. Royal College of Music, London. 28 August.

Knauer, Wolfram. 1990. "'Simulated Improvisation' in Duke Ellington's 'Black, Brown and Beige'." *The Black Perspective on Music*, 18, nos 1–2: 20–38.

Koestenbaum, Wayne. 1993. *The Queen's Throat: Opera, Homosexuality and the Mystery of Desire*. London: Penguin Books.

Krims, Adam. 2007. *Music and Urban Geography*. New York: Routledge.

Lacasse, Serge. 2000. "'Listen to My Voice': The Evocative Power of Vocal Staging in Recorded Rock Music and Other Forms of Vocal Expression." PhD dissertation, University of Liverpool.

Laing, Dave *et al.* 1975. *The Electric Muse: The Story of Folk into Rock*. London: Eyre Methuen.

Lake, Kirk. 2009. *There Will Be Rainbows: A Biography of Rufus Wainwright*. London: Orion Books.

La Rocca, Claudia. 2006. "Stephen Petronio Teams with Rufus Wainwright to Create 'Bloom', about Unjaded Youth." *New York Times*, 9 April. http://www.nytimes.com/2006/04/09/arts/dance/09laro.html?pagewanted=all&_r=0 (accessed 31 January 2014).

Locke, Ralph P. 1991. "Constructing the Oriental 'Other': Saint-Saëns's *Samson et Dalila*." *Cambridge Opera Journal* 3: 261–302.

Macdonald, Hugh. n.d. "Carmen (ii)." *Oxford Music Online*. http://www.oxfordmusiconline.com/subscriber/article/grove/music/O008315?q=bizet+l%27oiseau&search=quick&pos=3&_start=1#firsthit (accessed 4 June 2013).

McClary, Susan. 1992. *Georges Bizet: Carmen*. Cambridge: Cambridge University Press.

Metzer, David. 2003. *Quotation and Cultural Meaning in Twentieth-Century Music*. Cambridge: Cambridge University Press.

Monson, Ingrid. 1996. *Saying Something: Jazz Improvisation and Interaction*. Chicago: University of Chicago Press.

Moore, Allan F. 2001. *Rock: The Primary Text: Developing a Musicology of Rock*, 2nd edn. Aldershot: Ashgate.

—2002. "Authenticity as Authentication." *Popular Music* 21, no. 2: 209–223.

—2010. "Where is Here? An Issue of Deictic Projection in Recorded Song." *Journal of the Royal Musical Association* 135, no. 1: 145–82.

—2012. *Song Means: Analysing and Interpreting Recorded Popular Song*. Farnham: Ashgate.

Moore, Allan, Patricia Schmidt and Ruth Dockwray. 2009. "A Hermeneutics of Spatialization for Recorded Song." *Twentieth-century Music* 6, no. 1: 83–114.

Nemeth, Tisha. n.d. "Cool Cleveland interviews Rufus Wainwright." http://cool.coolcleveland.com/wiki/Newsletter/CoolClevelandInterviewsRufusWainwright (accessed 22 October 2015).

Patalono, Heidi. 2013. "Inside Gramercy Park with Rufus Wainwright." *DNAinfo*, New York, 4 June. http://www.dnainfo.com/new-york/20130604/gramercy/inside-gramercy-park-with-rufus-wainwright (accessed 2 July 2014).

Potter, Keith. 2000. *Four Musical Minimalists: La Monte Young, Terry Riley, Steve Reich, Philip Glass*. Cambridge: Cambridge University Press.

Robinson, John. 2005. "Rufus Wainwright: Poses." *New Music Express*, 12 September. http://www.nme.com/reviews/rufus-wainwright/5180 (accessed 2 July 2015).

Robinson, Paul. 1994. "The Opera Queen: A Voice from the Closet." *Cambridge Opera Journal* 6, no. 3 (November): 283–91.

Robinson, Peter. 1992. "Merimée's *Carmen*," 1–14. Introduction to Susan McClary, *Georges Bizet: Carmen*. Cambridge: Cambridge University Press.

Rosenburg, Ned V., ed. 1993. *Transforming Tradition: Folk Music Revivals Examined*. Urbana: University of Illinois Press.

Schruers, Fred. 1999. "Fathers and Sons." *Rolling Stone* 825: 61–94.

Schwandt, Kevin C. 2010. "'Oh What a World': Queer Masculinities, the Musical Construction of a Reparative Cultural Historiography and the Music of Rufus Wainwright." PhD thesis, University of Minnesota.

Scott, George, dir. 2005. *Rufus Wainwright: All I Want*. 200 mins. Universal Music DVD Video. USA.

—2009. *Rufus Wainwright. Prima Donna: The Story of an Opera*. 84 mins. Decca Music Group Limited. USA.

Shaitly, Shahesta. 2014. "Rufus Wainwright: 'Coming out to my parents was a nightmare'." *The Guardian*, 1 March.

Small, Christopher. 1998. *Musicking: The Meaning of Performing and Listening*. Middletown, CT: Wesleyan University Press.

Smith, Oliver C. E. 2013. "'The Cult of the Diva': Rufus Wainwright as Opera Queen." *Transpositions: musiques et science sociales* 3 (March). http://transposition-revue.org/The-Cult-of-the-Diva-Rufus?lang=fr#nb4 (accessed 2 July 2014).

Solie, Ruth A., ed. 1995. *Musicology and Difference: Gender and Sexuality in Music Scholarship*. Berkeley and Los Angeles: University of California Press.

Solomon, Maynard. 1989. "Franz Schubert and the Peacocks of Benvenuto Cellini." *Nineteenth Century Music* 12: 193–206.

Steblin, Rita. 1992. "Franz Schubert und das Ehe-Consense Gesetz von 1815." *Schubert durch die Brille* 9: 32–42.

—1993. "The Peacock's Tale: Schubert's Sexuality Reconsidered." *19th-Century Music* 17: 3–33.

Sturges, Fiona. 2012. "Who's the Daddy?" *The Independent on Sunday*. 15 April.

Swift, Jacqui. 2012. "I've Conquered Opera, Done Judy Garland, Now I Want to be a Pop Star." *The Sun*, 9 March. http://www.thesun.co.uk/sol/homepage/showbiz/sftw/4182361/Ive-conquered-opera-done-Judy-Garland-now-I-want-to-be-a-pop-star.html (accessed 11 June 2014).

Tommasini, Anthony. 2005. "Born into Popular Music, Weaned on Opera." *New York Times*, 7 September.

Troussé, Stephen. 2011. "House of Rufus Review." *Uncut*, 25 July. http://www.uncut.co.uk/rufus-wainwright/rufus-wainwright-house-of-rufus-review (accessed 14 January 2013).

Vaziri, Aidin. 2012. "Rufus Wainwright's Family Christmas." *San Francisco Chronicle*, 16 December. http://www.sfgate.com/music/popquiz/article/Rufus-Wainwright-s-family-Christmas-4116906.php (accessed 20 December 2012).

Wainwright, Rufus. 2003. *Want One* press materials. DreamWorks Records.

—2012. Preface to *Songs for Lulu for Voice and Piano*. New York: Schott.

Watercutter, Angela. 2011. "Tori Amos goes Centuries-Old-School on New Album Night of Hunters." *Wired*. http://www.wired.com/2011/09/tori-amos-night-of-hunters (accessed 29 October 2015).

Whiteley, Sheila, Andy Bennett and Stan Hawkins, eds. 2004. *Music, Space and Place: Popular Music and Cultural Identity*. Aldershot: Ashgate.

Whyton, Tony. 2010. *Jazz Icons: Heroes, Myths and the Jazz Tradition*. Cambridge: Cambridge University Press.

Williams, Justin A. 2010. "'You never been on a ride like this befo': Los Angeles, Automotive Listening, and Dr. Dre's 'G-Funk'." *Popular Music History* 4, no. 2: 160–76.

Williams, Justin, and Ross Wilson. 2016. "Music and Crowdfunded Websites: Digital Patronage and Artist-Fan Interactivity." *Music and Virtuality* (forthcoming).

Williams, Katherine. 2012a. "Valuing Jazz: Cross-cultural Comparisons of the Classical Influence in Jazz." PhD dissertation, University of Nottingham. http://etheses.nottingham.ac.uk/2622/ (accessed 24 March 2014).

—2012b. "Improvisation as Composition: Fixity of Form and Collaborative Composition in Duke Ellington's *Diminuendo and Crescendo in Blue*." *Jazz Perspectives* 6, nos 1–2: 223–46.

—2013. "Post-World War II Jazz in Britain: Venues and Values 1945–1970." *Jazz Research Journal* 7, no. 1: 113–31.

Youens, Susan. 1997. "Schubert and his Poets: Issues and Conundrums." In *The Cambridge Companion to Schubert*, ed. Christopher H. Gibbs, 99–120. Cambridge: Cambridge University Press.

Scores

Schubert, Franz. 'Ave Maria!' Neue Ausgabe sämtlicher Werke. *Serie IV: Lieder. Band 3*. Bärenreiter-Verlag Kassel: Basel/London, BA 5519.

Wainwright, Rufus. 'Pretty Things.' WB Music Cops and Put Tit On Music, 2003.

—*Prima Donna*. Jardin Cour and WB Music, 2009. Dramatic rights represented by Schott Music Company.

Filmography

I Could Go On Singing, dir. Ronald Neame. 99 mins. United Artists/Metro Goldwyn Mayer, 1963.

Imagine: Alan Yentob and Rufus Wainwright. 50 mins. First aired BBC1, 7 July 2009.

Rufus! Rufus! Rufus! Does Judy! Judy! Judy! 132 mins. 3DD Productions Limited and Geffen Records. Audio mixed by Frank Filipetti. 2007.

Rufus Wainwright: All I Want, dir. George Scott. 200 mins. Universal Music DVD Video. USA, 2005.

Rufus Wainwright. Prima Donna: The Story of an Opera, dir. George Scott. 84 mins. Decca Music Group Limited. USA, 2009.

Secrets of the Pop Song: Ballad (Part 1). 59 mins. First aired BBC2, 2 July 2011.
Sing Me The Songs That Say I Love You: A Concert for Kate McGarrigle, dir. Liam Lunson. 105
    mins. Horse Pictures. USA, 2012.
The Callas Conversations. Volumes 1 and 2. BBC, 1968.

Discography

Kate McGarrigle

Kate and Anna McGarrigle. Warner Brothers. 1975.
Dancer with Bruised Knees. Warner Brothers. 1975.
Pronto Monto. Warner Brothers. 1978.
Entre Lajeunesse et la Sagesse/French Record. Kébec-Disc. 1980.
Love Over and Over. Polydor Records. 1982.
Heartbeats Accelerating. Private Records. 1990.
Matapédia. Hannibal Records. 1996.
The McGarrigle Hour. Hannibal Records. 1998.
La vache qui pleure. La Tribu. 2003.
The McGarrigle Christmas Hour. Nonesuch. 2005.

Loudon Wainwright III

Loudon Wainwright III. Atlantic. 1970.
Album II. Atlantic. 1971.
Album III. Columbia. 1973.
Attempted Mustache. Columbia. 1975.
Unrequited. Columbia. 1975.
T-Shirt. Arista Records. 1976.
A Live One. Self-produced. 1979.
Fame and Wealth. Rounder. 1983.
I'm Alright. Rounder. 1985.
More Love Songs. Rounder. 1986.
Therapy. Silvertone. 1989.
History. Charisma. 1992.
Career Moves. Virgin. 1993.
Grown Man. Virgin. 1995.
Little Ship. Virgin/Charisma. 1997.
BBC Sessions. BBC. 1998.
Social Studies. Hannibal. 1999.
Last Man on Earth. Red House. 2001.
So Damn Happy. Sanctuary. 2003.
Here Come the Choppers. Sovereign Records. 2005.
Strange Weirdos. Concord. 2007.
Recovery. Yep Roc. 2008.
High, Wide & Handsome: The Charlie Poole Project. 2nd Story Sound. 2009.
10 Songs for the New Depression. Proper. 2010.
Older Than My Old Man Now. 2nd Story Sound. 2012.

Martha Wainwright

Martha Wainwright. MapleMusic, Zöe Records. 2005.
I Know You're Married But I've Got Feelings Too. MapleMusic, Zöe Records. 2008.
Sans Fusils, Ni Souliers, à Paris: Martha Wainwright's Piaf Record. MapleMusic, V2 Records. 2009.
Come Home to Mama. V2 Records. 2012.

Rufus Wainwright

Rufus Wainwright. DreamWorks Records. 1998.
Poses. DreamWorks Records. 2001.
Want One. DreamWorks Records. 2003.
Want Two. DreamWorks Records. 2004.
Release the Stars. Geffen Records. 2007.
All Days are Nights: Songs for Lulu. Decca Records. 2010.
Out of the Game. Decca Records. 2012.
Yellow Lounge Compiled by Rufus Wainwright. Deutsche Grammophon. 2007.
Various Artists. *Sing Me The Songs: Celebrating the Work of Kate McGarrigle*. Nonesuch Records Inc./Warner Music Group Company. 2013.

Other

Amos, Tori. *Night of Hunters*. Deutsche Grammophon. 2011.
Garland, Judy. *Judy! Judy! Judy! At Carnegie Hall in Person*. Capitol Records, 1961.
Parks, Van Dyke. *Song Cycle*. Warner Bros. Records, 1967.

Index

Lightning Source UK Ltd.
Milton Keynes UK
UKOW06n0704280116

267237UK00001B/26/P